Unfortunately I Am Schizophrenic

(In today's Irish and British culture)

Edition – 2

RICHARD MAGEE

Dedication

My Wonderful Mother, Eileen Magee, who stood by me like a rock at all times.

"I thought of the voices as… something a little different from aliens. I thought of them more like angels … It's really my subconscious talking, it was really that… I know that now."

– John Forbes Nash, Jr.

ISBN 9798389780064

About the Author

Richard Magee is a two-time Published Author. "The Mood Swings" (an amazing read) was his first publication and the second, "Where Were You Jesus?"

'Where were you Jesus?' is a fascinating insight into how the author approaches his late teens with optimism until the dark periods encroached upon his daily life. As these epochs increased in frequency and strength. Richard gradually lost the ability to cope until, finally, feeling helpless in America, Richard returned home to Ireland only to be diagnosed with schizophrenia.

In "Unfortunately I am Schizophrenic" Richard Magee takes the reader along a journey of one man's lifetime struggle with mental health issues. Richard has candidly penned an eye-opening saga affected by schizophrenia. He intensely describes how the condition and the drugs used to combat it (not very effective in the early 90s), really affected his ability to function and overall health. He outlines how the system failed to pay attention, burdening it further with tons and tons of medication; resulting in a kind of contradiction of normality.

Written in an engaging and authentic elegance and a grain of the Irish humour, Richard precisely empathizes with all those who are in some way afflicted by similar ailment.

When someone like Richard puts so much of himself into words for the world to see, then the least, we owe him is gratitude for having the resolve and courage to do so. “Unfortunately I am Schizophrenic”, while not a candidate for the booker prize, is surely worth a read.

Table of Contents

Introduction

I have not been a psychotic person for the last ten years, but I definitely had psychosis. And when I was in America on a student visa, I wasn't able to deal with my psychosis *(and diagnosis of paranoia schizophrenia)* like a regular mental health patient.

I arrived in New York in 1987 with no medication whatsoever, totally paranoid, shaking and sweating and a nervous wreck. My three friends didn't realise it as they were young. None of my mates in college comprehended it either, not a single person in college recognized its gravity. I was Richie, the gas man, the stand-up comic, the party animal – but that was all sometime around June 1986.

And then one year later, it was the totally psychotic, severely mentally ill person who needed medication, hospitalisation, rest, quiet, counselling and literally tons and tons of anti-psychotic pills in order to cope.

The gas man was gone…

I arrived in New York frightened *(like thousands of other students)* in the throes of a developing nervous breakdown. It was up to me to sink or swim. And I decided to swim.

We are Great

Do you know if you meet somebody who has lived with schizophrenia for years, instead of being an arsehole like racist people are *(you should embrace culture change and difference),* you should shake the schizophrenic sufferers' hands and congratulate them for still being alive and coping with one of the worst, most dreadfully pain-inducing, torturing, agonising conditions ever known to man. You should thank God or Heaven that you don't suffer with this 'chronic and life-enduring' mental health condition that schizophrenia is.

And the fact is that so many sufferers commit suicide because of this illness. And society, along with the doctors, don't care much about us except for the odd one. Most doctors don't even read the product authorisation sheets in our boxes of medication.

The True Delusion

To me, I poisoned the blood in my brain years ago with hash and I think of my brain as being inferior to the brain of a person who never smoked hash. But all things said, I'm very lucky because I only have to deal with this false belief for maybe ten minutes and some days not at all. And in reality, the only brain damage I have is the damage I do to myself thinking about this idea and trying to rationalise, whereby it just returns five minutes later and I have to do it all over again and then again and again until I am nearly driven insane.

Mentally well people are very balanced and even if I am unwell, they know I'll always have this delusion but that I can live with it most of the time. But to have it is an extremely tough struggle. I learnt about medication and I couldn't care less what any Christian tells about the negative effects: because 'medication' is the definite way to at least open a channel of healing the mind.

In My Defence

I know in the normal course of events that a man should not go to prostitutes and if I didn't have schizophrenia and if I had a chance to meet someone and have a relationship with them, I wouldn't have gone to them. But I tried and tried to meet someone.

I tried from all angles to be as polite and complimentary as I could. I was sometimes over-friendly, and other times I was not. I decided that it was not worth it because it made no difference. I was fobbed off and scammed regularly….

I felt enormous discomfort when I saw my friends getting happy and satisfied with all the blessings a person could possibly dream of. Whereas nobody was interested in me and while I'm not a film star, I'm not even ugly looking.

Now I realise it was not God's Will. But at the time I felt huge pain of watching my mates carrying on. It would never happen for me and I had even accepted it and yet it was sad and very lonely at times.

I often wonder how millions of people who suffer with far worse conditions cope with life? But schizophrenia is a road that is harder to negotiate than the average person's life. "What can I do?" I had asked my counsellor. "I haven't had a kiss or a hug in fifteen years." I said with anger and frustration. My counsellor would always be considerate of my feelings – she always heard me.

So many questions haunted my mind…

I wouldn't even harm a fly; *then why do I deserve to be alone?* Apart from a bit of companionship, which I am very grateful for, I am completely sex-starved and would love to be in a relationship. I know several women will be disgusted to read this but I have the money and I'm going to go to escorts. You tell me, what other choice do I have? Can you wear my shoes for even a moment? Women may be angry but I'm upset too!! I'd never have gone near a trafficked girl. The ones I went to always told me they enjoyed it and also made good money.

I understand you. All I request you is to also understand me and people like me. Our woes are not easy…

Thanks very much.

The Mentally Ill

Patrick's Pain

Even on cold winter days, Patrick used to sit out under the ledge of the workshop window of the potting shed. He'd sit there shivering on his hunkers and time just passed like a blur for him. Or so people thought. He wasn't well enough to work but he battled away with his thoughts and his delusions, paranoia and anxiety.

He was trying to rationalise everything, only for when he had sorted it out in his mind, then it would return and start again, i.e. his nagging thoughts. He had plenty to occupy him. The workers in the garden used to stop and say hello to him when they were passing in and out with the wheel barrows of builders' sand or soil and potted plants for the garden.

The garden was a secluded walled Victorian garden and there was no pressure on people to work too hard. Sadly we didn't have to, some complained, but we were all trying to cope to a greater or lesser extent with schizophrenia.

Sometimes Patrick would cackle away laughing at a joke you'd tell him. Other days he just stared at the horizon in agony it seemed.

"How are you coping Patrick?" I asked as I passed by him with a wheel barrow loaded with plants.

"How are you feeling today?" I rephrased my concern. His face strained as he tried to answer the question and flushed as he did his best trying to hide his internal psychological agony.

"Not too bad." he muttered. "I'm doing my best." He made an effort to smile.

"Would you like to hear a joke?" I asked thinking it might distract him. But he wasn't in the mood for a joke.

"No thanks." He said, "it's a tough day today."

"I understand Patrick." I said. "Maybe tomorrow!"

"Maybe then…" he'd wince. It was nearly 3.30pm. "Safe home." I said, "have a good evening." But I knew he wouldn't. He was suffering and would suffer for many years. It's very sad but he was very ill.

In the afternoon at 3.30pm, the hospital van would arrive and collect the resident hospital patients from

Grove Hall and take them back. Patrick always sat at the back of the bus for some reason, as all the mentally ill would head back for their evening dose of medication. Why did God invent schizophrenia?

Patrick arrived back at the hospital after saying goodbye to me at the cherry house gardens. He got out of the back of the bus and went into the hospital corridor. He was generally very ill; however he had definitely improved since the winter months. It was now mid-May.

In February, he had spent long evenings walking up and down the corridor shuffling his feet and saying out loud; 'I have my faith - I have I have my faith.' There were two other patients who trawled the corridors with him, both praying out loud. The poor receptionist observed them for hours on end from her desk. I remember observing these two gentlemen six years earlier doing the same thing and neither of them seemed to have improved at all in six years. I was now trying to understand my mother's explanation to my two brothers that, 'suffering is part of the human condition.'

People seemed to be battling with hell in here in the hospital. Patrick was fighting an internal war and his doctors knew about his delusions but nobody else did. This was because he was a very private person and suffered in silence. I suffered with delusions also but I had some respite from them and if I didn't drink Coffee, I would have days where my illness would leave me alone completely. With Patrick, this did not seem to be the case. It seemed that even God was at a loss to help him as much as possible as his brain disease was so severe.

In those days, mindfulness and meditation were not practised to help the mentally ill. He used to pray a lot, but that was an active pastime, whereas he needed to switch off. He was so brave, as he could not concentrate on anything. But he trusted God. He wouldn't give up. He would climb the mountain. He would try to regain his health whereas others would just commit suicide.

Mark

He was lonely and suicidal and unable to walk properly and he was angry with his parents and sick of life and he just wanted to die.

"I'll show my mother and father, I'll show them - I will. They're going to Sligo to live and they're leaving me in Dublin. They don't care, they just want to head off and leave Dublin and they don't want me to come with them."

"I asked if I could come? I said I would try to get a job over in Sligo, and ye know what? I'll fucking show them."

"But you did make yourself unwell Mark," I said. "By meeting Paddy X and smoking hash. Surely you realise hash is lethal for our illness?"

"I didn't want to be the odd one out and I didn't want to let them down." Said Mark.

"Fuck not letting them down Mark," I said. "You have an illness, you're schizophrenic and you let them make you smoke hash!" I was filled with rage. "Did that bastard have any cop on?" I continued.

They had all been out with the crowd from the labelling and packaging company in Magnums in Dun Laoghaire, drinking. In those days you could smoke in a pub and a nightclub. Hash was going around.

"Paddy, Mark has head problems, he can try hash if he wants but we're doing mushrooms." said Jimmy.

"Do you really think we should let Mark take the mushrooms Paddy?" Jimmy asked.

"Just tell Mark to chill and relax, he can take the mushrooms," said Paddy.

Mark spent the last two years of his life in front of the altar in the Sacrament Chapel in 'St. John of God hospital.' When he got out of hospital, the doctors sent him back to work. He was living in a flat in Rathmines.

He took an overdose and went for a run. When the drugs kicked in, he ran by the Dodder canal and threw himself into the water and drowned…

When Everyone Else is Happy & Well

When I was becoming ill, things like holding a conversation and trying to laugh and just to be spontaneous and relaxed seemed like arduous tasks, far from easy.

I looked around me and everyone was able to drink alcohol and enjoy it. Everyone was able to look at the other person in the eye and have a conversation without feeling a rush of anxiety or nervousness or simply incapable of telling a joke, the way I was able to – only a few months ago.

I thought this was happening to everyone else. I supposed that there was nothing wrong with me and that I was just unhappy - until I got worse and worse… Soon, I realised I was feeling extremely ill. I didn't know how to stop it. I didn't even realise I was schizophrenic and that most people never experience this and how uncool and anti-social it appears when you are mentally ill but I just couldn't do anything about it; hence my condition kept going from bad to worse.

My heart had dreams but little did it know that those were soon to be shattered as I was heading towards a mental breakdown. My life was about to get topsy-turvy, visions were to be converted into delusions. I was beginning to feel minor streaks of depression and anxiety off and on. And dark thoughts; when I really had to put in an effort and make-believe that the sun was always shining, even when I couldn't see it at times. I was twenty plus and I began to feel like 50 plus every so often.

I was becoming extremely sensitive. It was becoming harder and harder to crack a joke or be spontaneous about it. The more I tried to shrug these thoughts off, the more they followed me. And yet, I kept reassuring myself that there was nothing wrong with me, not knowing what was about to come.

My life wasn't going to be as I thought - My mind was going to have an unanticipated guest that wasn't going to leave soon…

As Michael Chabon said:

"Man makes plans…and God laughs"

Slipping My 21st Birthday

"Go on, Rich," said Niall. "Get up there and tell us a few jokes!"

At this stage of the year (May 1987), my nerves were truly shot and I was finding it hard to concentrate on what I was doing or saying.

Simon Dooley, a lovely chap from county Laois, and I had arranged to have our 21st birthday parties together in the Little Owl pub in Dublin street in Carlow. He was a month younger than me but we decided to have the party in between the two dates, on April the 12th.

"God," he said, "I am really looking forward to this - it'll be some craic." He added.

"Yes, it will be, Simon," I said, wondering how in the name of God I was going to get through the night not knowing what was happening to me.

Somehow or other, we got through organising the party, which then had me in a better mood. However, I could not understand why I was so withdrawn and why I felt so nervous. I was saying to myself;

'Snap out of it, Rich, you are young, just stop being depressed and think positive.'

But all the time, I was anxious, sweaty, my neck sore from tension and I was growing even more paranoid and irritated every day. I was also becoming scruffy and not washing myself regularly.

The interesting part is I had my own room in a shared house, with a big poster of a young Bono on stage in Croke Park.

"What's going on with ye, Bono, is that a dye job on your hair?"

"Well, you didn't like the old me, so I found someone new."

"Isn't it a bit self-indulgent to look like that, so cool, on a huge screen?"

"It does, absolutely – but you look great…" *(as he puffed on a cigar and smiled).*

I was changing.

The party went extremely well for most people.

"Some craic it was!" said Pat.

"Brilliant," said Simon. "Did you enjoy it Rich?"

"Ah … yeah, I did…" I struggled to say.

We were due to go to the USA on J1 student visas in three weeks, all four of us. I was 21 and they were nearly 20.

The lads must have been wondering what in the name of God was wrong with me;

- I was visibly grey in the face,
- I could not make eye contact,
- I couldn't laugh,
- My tone of voice had died,
- I felt shaken all the time,
- Even though I was sleeping well; I felt awful.

"You look shattered, Richard." When I was on a bus and someone laughed out loud, I usually thought I was the target. After a good night's sleep … I woke up to … immediately and without logic - my demons.

'What the fuck is happening to me?'

One Sunday night before we left for the USA, I went to the Samaritans in Dublin, on the way back to college. It was about 8PM. On the Quays, they opened the big, dark, grey door and told me to come in.

"Karen will be with you in a minute."

I poured out my heart to Karen, telling her I was very depressed, nervous and upset.

"What reason can you give for feeling like this?" she said and advised me to: "Keep batting. Keep batting. You are doing fine; you just need to be more positive."

Obviously, like all the students in college, not one of them without exception knew I was having a nervous breakdown.

Schizophrenia, Is that You?

I would cry all the time, but not as badly as I had done in America. The doctors couldn't believe I'd been in America for five months! Five months… totally psychotic and not one tablet for a month until Dr Jacoby gave me anti-depressants – I think he saved my life!

I was in a frighteningly dangerous city which wasn't even relatively safe then (1987).

I could not concentrate, I perspired buckets all the time. My heart hammered hard constantly. My neck was jarred stiff with anxiety and my hands shook all the time. The thoughts in my head went ten million miles an hour and nag, nag, nagged.

I wondered if there was anyone anywhere in the city or in any town or any other city in the world who felt as totally terrified as I did? And who felt they were going to vomit every five minutes. I couldn't even make eye contact with people. I couldn't understand the meaning of sentences spoken to me. I wouldn't laugh or smile. It was impossible. I found nothing even remotely amusing, albeit a very funny joke. The only sense that I had all day long was despair, nervousness or obsession; constantly tapping away at my head like a woodpecker. It was far from the conventional life that I had desired!

I had sensations of panic and anxiety every five minutes. Every conversation sounded like a drawl and made no sense to me. I couldn't ascertain the difference between humour and serious conversation. I knew that, logically, the joke was funny to a 'well' person. But I was seriously ill much more than I thought at that time.

***

I was very, very, very ill and here I was three thousand miles from home with only three hundred dollars in my pocket. And I simply had to get a job to eat and pay rent *(wherever Niall, Eamon, and I ended up.)*

We had to get jobs and luckily to God and all saints in heaven, I didn't realise that I was suffering from severe paranoid schizophrenia, and that I needed to be in a hospital. I didn't know this until I met Dr Jacoby and he suggested that I go back home. Dr Jacoby told me that private hospitals in New York (at the time) cost seven and a half thousand dollars a week. I mentioned to him that I could go to a public mental institute, but he said, "Magee, those places are not safe. You could be cut or chopped up within a week."

I bawled at him and asked if he could give me some tablets. He agreed and gave me anti-depressants. When he gave me those, I thought I would be fine for the rest of the summer... They did help to boost my mood but only for ten weeks... After that, all hell broke loose and I became psychotic.

***

"It's a brain disease, Richard..." She said to me as I let the tears flow.

"You'll always have it, but it can be controlled. You can live a normal life." Damien *(the nurse)* was looking across at me as Kathleen spoke.

"You'll have to take your medication, but you'll improve," she said trying to sound compassionate.

'At least, I am not in pain, I am not in physical agony.' I thought through my frightened faintness. I was frightened all the time and severely depressed.

Schizophrenia, is that you...?

Fear

I was playing tennis in Carrickmines at the club's team tennis tournament under the lights.

It was 9:30 pm and my eyesight was blurred, both from the medication and the pure anxiety I was suffering from. It was a doubles match. I kept thinking that some dreadful event that I would not be able to handle would happen.

"Fifteen all!" Sally Smith shouted.

"Richard, you are standing on the wrong side of the court," she added. "It's fifteen all. You are serving to me."

"Sorry, Sally," I said, shuffling to the other side of the court to serve.

Not one first serve was going in, as I was so nervous and under-confident. I kept getting a wobbly arm every time I served.

I was getting stressed from this.

'Come on, Rich', I said to myself – *'slow down! Take it easy. Focus on what you are doing.'*

The damned medication, plus the anxiety, had me struggling to get any serves in at all.

Damn it! Another double fault. I was playing with Mick Stubbles (mixed doubles), and he and I were way better than our opponents, but we were not doing ourselves justice. And we were 5 2 down in the first set.

I would have to learn to find coping mechanisms for my anxiety, but it was the early days of my illness, and I was doing the best I could.

Dancing with Delusion

I must be a very special person to have been chosen for such a special illness. Some people may have been entertained enough to see me quirky when my delusions got the best of me but when it didn't, I would fret about it all the time giving them all the more probability to laugh. But I'll tell you what; all the anti-psychotic medications that I have been given have side effects and the ones that worry me the most are weight gain and general fatigue. Although they may haunt me at various phases of my life but I would still have to take them all my life, or else I would end up dead or extremely ill. Anyone that I know with schizophrenia, who has come off the medication is either gone crazy or has committed suicide.

The medication that I have to take, keeps me alive but on some days, leaves me with no energy whatsoever. Most of the days, I fight my craving for coffee as caffeine helps quite a bit to get up and do something, something that I can and I love to. But then again, the joy of having that energy blurs in no time;

leaving me to dance with my delusions and that too with no music…

For most of you, the delusions that I live with must only be a thing you must have either read in books or seen in movies *(only if there were any ever made on schizophrenia struggles).* Often, I have to go through it despite taking my medication; and that's thanks to the crime of drinking a cup of coffee…! It's not really easy and also hard to describe in the exact words; being restless all the time, and pacing and moving without really having the energy to do it. It's impossible to get anything done such as writing in my journal or typing on a computer, leave alone having a regular job, a loving and long-term companion and just be simply happy. It's almost as if a demon is terrorizing you.

No number of words can accurately define what delusions are like. All I can say to best explain is; imagine hundreds of snakes crawling under your bed when you're lying down and you continuously feel it wiggle and vibrate. When you know that the chair or the bed did not actually move and that touching it, you wouldn't feel a thing, but you still feel that way in your head.

It might really sound amusing; but I'll tell you what; it's NOT!

The Foolish Quacks

If I was having a bad day and it continued for a few days and I couldn't summon up any positivity, I would stuff myself with anti-depressants to get over the bad days.

The drug I am on is Lexapro (10mg), which is a great anti-depressant and can lift your mood within three hours. You can go from being quite depressed to being in great form by just taking a couple of those (two or three). The illness may be impossible to live with at times, but the alternate for many has been suicide. As a friend of mine Christie (who swims in the Forty Foot) said about suicide:

It's a permanent solution to a temporary problem. And if the services had more counsellors, a lot fewer sufferers would commit suicide.

Doctors pretend they care about you. However, the last social care worker I had did his best and was kind, albeit ineffective and incapable of helping us much.

One day I was talking to my doctor about it.

"That's what I do," I said. "And I don't give a damn. You doctors don't have to live with this disease and you don't know how lucky you are!"

"And where do you get the extra tablets Richard?". She enquired.

"I have my sources," I said "and I'll never tell you, but I get the extra ones." was my only response.

Sometimes to escape from depression, I take a few extra antidepressants and enjoy the semi-euphoric feeling it gives. The doctors would be furious when they knew - but I really don't care. they don't have to live with mental illness and lots of them have no interest in us at all. To them, it's just a job with a nice hefty salary.

***

These fucking shrinks with their bullshit theories and registrars, total idiots, asking you about your bowels. Arrogant patronising little registrars of about 20 years of age, who think they understand 'mental illness.'

Half the time, the doctors don't even know what they're doing - not to mind the fucking registrars.

During the lockdown a couple of years ago, thanks to the historic pandemic Covid-19, people with mental health problems were now not only economically relegated, but also socially marginalised.

All these 40+ bastards with their cars and two kids and their yuppie wives were now beginning to feel the pain they may not have imagined before. They were all now talking about their mental health and the economic pressure!

blah – blah – blah – My ass!

They did not for a second, give a thought to how we survived even before the pandemic!

Let me put a simple question forward, meant for those high-class normal people – 'How would you like to live on €190 a week for 20 years and be treated like a complete idiot by the patronising – uncaring – indifferent psychiatrists, treating us *(ones with mental difficulties but also human beings)*, like we're stupid just because we have an illness? And every time we relaxed and smiled, *(after 20 years of struggling to be marginally spontaneous)* there they were only to tell us that we are high or elated.

"Richard, you are smiling today, do you normally talk that quickly when you are in good form? Are you a bit high?"

"I'm not high; I'm just having a good day. Something we don't have as much as you sure have!"

"I'm just doing my job."

"Then do it properly."

These arseholes earn €190,000 a year while a service user has to scrape by on merely €9,000 with no chance of work whatsoever, and you have all these clowns – *the so-called social workers* who meet you for coffee and pretend they are all about you; although they'd never in their wildest thoughts consider helping you get a Community Employment Scheme or a job for that matter.

When you go to your appointment with them, they never ask you anything about your personal life in general. It's all merely 'bullshit talk.'

"I am very proud of you; you have a lot going on Richard; and you know I am there for you."

"If you care, could you write a few letters to the government to get Community Employment Schemes back – to give people like some structure in their lives?"

"Oh, that is not in my remit."

They let the sufferers lie in bed all day because they know *there is really nothing that they can do for them on the job front.* They even admit that it's patronising to go to the day centres to play cards after fifteen or twenty years of your life - just trying to get better.

The illness does linger for a long time and the doctors don't tell you this because they know that loads of people won't make it, if they tell them this very truth.

By and large the whole mental health industry is a money-minting business where patients are just the pawns; simply manipulated in a nonessential method. They are stuffed to the gills with antipsychotic medicines to swell their *(the medics)* prescriptions. *(Mind you I know I was irresponsible myself previously.)*

Doctor Joe Soap is off swanning about on another junket or conference. It's quite similar to the supply and demand theory – where the price of a product rests on its obtainability and the customers' demand. The higher the fee of the product *(in this case, the medicine/prescription)* the better the supply! The business community must have determined what I'm trying to say here. In layman's term, we *(the patients)* are 'the product'.

As the drug companies *(several)* try to convince the psychiatrists to use their particular products. While were looking to have the drugs, we don't always need a prescription but we do sometimes need a conversation with the doctor!

Reckoning

Surely, working with mentally ill people ought to be more than a job, it ought to be a vocation.

What can we do.?

I was talking to Gerry one day at a social Clubhouse.

“I’m retired,” he said and he was only 48.

“I’m not putting myself through the stress of a proper job”.

“I agree.” I said. “Is it worth it with our illness?”

“No.” We both agreed.

“Do you ever get racing thoughts and do you ever feel as if your brain is flying?” I asked.

“Ah stop Rich…” he said. “Yes indeed I do.” He said with a big sigh.

“And we can’t marry and have kids. Also we can’t hold down a proper job.” He spoke with such sadness.

“I can!” I said. “I worked in America extremely ill for 22 weeks. I think we end up with our tails between our legs because we spend years thinking about our condition.”

“True Rich!” Gerry said and then took a large drag of his banana flavoured e cigarette.

“All we can do Rich is battle on…” He said honestly.

“Yes true.” I agreed. “But there isn’t enough done for people by the doctors. You’re just a number to them. There isn’t any cheap counselling. The doctors don’t seem to care.”

The Mentally ill people are often very confused and extremely frightened. The medication can take years to work and often doesn’t work at all. I also fully realise that the mental health staff have their own personal problems and stresses and sadly sometimes a mentally ailing person may not or cannot realise this; due to his/her own quandary.

Nonetheless, some also do recover and then they are often very kind because they have suffered and know exactly what suffering is like.

You know better – You do better

But the bigger question is; where is the compensation for families of suicide victims? Surely, if a patient is being monitored properly, this should not happen. If this was the United States, hundreds of doctors would be sued.

EVERY LIFE MATTERS!

Just to say though that there are some very good doctors, but not many and also we need occupation but we can’t work fulltime as it’s too stressful.

Why Won't it Happen For Me?

I watched all my mates in jobs, dating girls and soon getting married. While I was three stone overweight and looked exhausted all the time. I had a dry mouth with food stuck to my lips due to Mellaril. And I became a wreck, trying to talk to girls…

I prayed… One Day… I'd meet someone…

'Why is it,' *(I thought to myself)* 'that people with my illness can never seem to meet someone nice for a romantic relationship?'

I watched my mates falling into romantic relationships and yet it wouldn't happen for me.

I met girls when I went out but my self-esteem collapsed after I got ill. Would anyone in their right mind stay alive if they realised that they'd have to deal with mental persecution and confusion and a constant feeling of being left outside by the crowd?

Going home to your flat alone every night while all your friends were going to their girlfriends or wives for the night, is an awful feeling. Most of the time fully 'well' people get through life far easier than schizophrenics. And the knowledge a schizophrenic has that his illness will never leave him or her is far too much for most people who suffer.

Edmund

He was a great doctor and a very understanding psychiatrist; kind, caring and a good listener.

I walked into his office after waiting twenty minutes in the anxiety ridden sweat shop *(that contained loads of sufferers all with anxiety or depression or psychosis).* That was the waiting room. Edmund was busy hammering out a letter on his old type writer.

"Have a seat," he said. "I'll be with you in a minute."

"Take your time." I said being in no rush. I had been dying to ask him all about my delusion but he knew better than I did; that it only feeds the idea the more you talk about.

"We won't talk about it," he said.

"Did you see the match last night Richard?" He countered to distract me from the thoughts. He was right to do that. Edmund was an avid Liverpool fan like I was.

"Yes." I said. "I watched it Doc, wasn't it a marvellous match. When Gerrard scored the third goal the place shook with the noise. Unbelievable! I knew he looked tired. So you were there??"

"Yes I was." He said.

'You corporate scumbag' – I thought to myself… 'On your salary you could bring all the patients in the hospital!!'

After around another twenty minutes of chat about football, he suddenly panicked and looked at his watch.

"God! the time!!" He exclaimed and then he looked at me and said, "do you need a prescription?"

"Yes." I said.

That was crucial but at least 'Edmund' would give you 40 or 50 minutes and if you needed to unload your problems, he'd let you do that.

A Medicated Stupor

Cormac and I were out in Howth, driving around and chatting and having a great laugh.

Those who aren't aware of 'Howth' - it is an Irish village on the Howth Peninsula, north of central Dublin.

I don't know if it was because of the place, atmosphere or our states of mind that we had this significant conversation, garnished by my sarcasm.

"Do you think there's a God, Cormac?" I asked. My incessant search for meaning continued.

"Oh yes, Rich." He said sarcastically.

"And where is he Cormac?" I asked.

"Oh, he's everywhere." He said grinning.

"He's beside us in the back seat here in the car, he's in the trees, he's in all the offices in Portobello…"

"But the offices are shut, Cormac." I said.

"Ah yes, but he just glides in and out through the locked door and into all the lobbies and then into the offices," he laughed.

"And he can fiddle the books, while he's there and make a few extra bob for himself!" I said.

God! Such sacrilege.

But the two of us needed to keep our sense of humour, as we were both in recovery from schizophrenia and we often had very little to laugh about.

I also felt very let down by God as I watched my friends live their lives, while I suffered all the time for the last five years and would in the future.

***

Cormac and I drove around Phibsboro in Dublin on a Friday night in the rain.

We both wondered where we were going in the car and where our lives were going. We both had endured twenty years of mental illness. We were both sad and disillusioned by life. Society didn't give a shit about us as we were too medicated to work.

I was stoned out of my face on nine hundred milligrams of Mellaril and persecuted by delusions which nagged at me all day long.

"The doctors don't give a shit about us, do they Cormac, do they??"

"What do you think?"

"No they don't care." I was sure.

Cormac sighed as he pulled into Phibsboro shopping centre and lit a cigarette.

"They changed my medication last week." he said. "And now I can't sleep!"

"Bloody bastards." I said. "They have no right to do that without consulting you about it and discussing it."

"No they never said a word about it." He said

"I just realised it when I went to take my medication, and they had increased the anti-psychotic which helps me to sleep."

"Typical shrinks." I thought.

The rest of the drive was in deafening silence…

The Registrar

When you're 24 years of age and terrified by anxiety and the nagging thoughts with terrifying solutions; you look around you… as did I.

But don't forget, I was schizophrenic – hence different. Even one of my best friends told me that I was different. This basically meant – I was never going to have a job, I was never going to fall in love, and the only way I could cope with my life was to remain a nobody and nowhere near reality.

For three years, I took nearly twice as much medication as I was prescribed. I took the piss out of the mental health services, getting a prescription from my psychiatrist and often one from my GP. I filled myself up to the eyeballs with medication. The situation was just about hopeless.

This next-to-useless Irish psychiatric system, which absolutely fails to understand.

I have previously been prescribed Mellaril by one of Ireland's so-called experts - who made a complete bollocks of my treatment at the age of 17. They never prescribed me any medication while I was in the early stages of psychosis. And then tried to rectify the situation when I was 21.

BUT the 'damage' was already done.

All these quacks understand is 'medication'.

They repeatedly treat their patients like total idiots. A brain disease often invites the little wankers *(the interns)* on call into the room and then you are at their mercy. Their job is to interview the unfortunate patient. They talk to the junior doctor about this subject and then talk at the patient. Patronising, insulting and heartless crew.

"Are you hearing any voices?"

"Do you think that people are putting thoughts into your head?"

And then to the kid;

"His/her concentration hastens rapidly today."

These bastards earn around €190,000 a year just for sitting around scratching their asses, frequently prescribing drugs that clash with each other; killing the power in the unfortunate schizophrenic or bipolar manic-depressive person.

Most of the doctors wouldn't give a shit about their patients, or have the time to even remember their names. Most of the times, they have to ask the attendant what medication is he or she prescribed in a month?! This is how disorganised they are and absolutely inept to care. How can they just not remember where the matter could be of life and death?

***

I walked into a small office on the third floor of Carlisle House. There, sitting down in the office, was this registrar. *The little bastard hadn't even the manners to stand up and shake hands or even to extend a hand and say hello.* This was before the Covid virus – way back in 2017.

I looked at him as he sat there *(the pompous prick)* and I estimated him to be just about 22 years old. He didn't even look up when I sat in the chair opposite him.

"Now…", he began to speak without even making any eye contact. "So … eh … how well are you?" He asked casually.

"My name is Richard by the way…" *(asshole).* "What's your name", I asked. *(I decided at this stage that I was going to take the piss out of this total gobshite).*

"My name is Doctor O'Brien."

I laughed; "ha ha, you're not a fucking doctor," I said. "You're 22 years old and you're a fuckin idiot; you didn't even say hello when I walked into the room, never crossed your mind! Did it, shit for brains?" I asked.

In my mind I'd wanted to say, 'you're about 17. I bet you, you have no hair on your bollox, and by the looks of it, you haven't even started shaving, have you? Eh? Arsehole!'

"What was that? Did you say something?"

I asked you a question! "I'd like to hear your answer." I said.

"I'm not answering that," said the poor pathetic little bastard.

"Well buddy," I said, "I'm not answering your questions either. Don't forget to go straight home at 5pm; your mummy will be waiting for you to give you your tea and you have to be in bed by 7pm or you won't grow up to be a big strong boy, will you?"

I didn't stop at that, adding, "you don't know anything about schizophrenia, or about our lives and you think we're idiots. Well, we are Not! You are the clown coming here, thinking you can talk down to us, you fucking wanker! When you know nothing about our lives; you just go to college and learn about us and don't come here thinking you can treat us like guinea pigs. So fuck yourself!" I said my say and without waiting a moment, slammed the door on my way out.

'Registrars are fucking arseholes.' My mind was repeating the very thought.

This is the modern psychiatry. *There is no interest for the agonized patients.* You just see their crucial faces for a while and then after that, they couldn't care less. Most of them couldn't even give a shit most of the time, blaming the 'County of Dublin' having no social worker for the patient.

My question is - how come there are no counsellors for us? One can only look forward to the 'pleasure' of seeing the quack again in three months for merely five minutes with a prescription for polypharmacy.

Mark Noble

Farewell to West Ham after 18 years

And there he was, Mark Noble; aged 38, retiring from professional soccer after 18 years. There he was with his wife and kids. His daughter was about 14 or 15 years old and his son was about 12 or 13 plus of course, his young and lovely wife.

And I felt the pain.

Thinking he was 18 years younger than me and he'd had a life. He had a lovely wife, a beautiful daughter. How very emotional as she watched her father being saluted by the thousands of West Ham fans who'd adored him for the last 15 to 16 years as he established himself as a top player in the premier league recently, under the stewardship of the excellent man manager and tactician David Moyes, who continuously improves teams wherever he goes.

I looked at my own fucked up life. Mentally ill on and off from the age of 17 and permanently ill since 21.

I wouldn't have been able to socialise with any of these fans or enjoy the craic with them *(as if I was a West fan!)* I'm a Liverpool fan – and that too for 26 fucking years. I wasn't well enough to go to Anfield *(football stadium)* and enjoy a match. Any chance of any career I hoped to have had been destroyed by my illness. I couldn't concentrate on anything for more than 25 seconds.

Thank you very much. Are You that heartless Jesus? Thanks so much for an even bash at life…

And thanks also for coming to the aid of the Ukrainian people in their hour of agony…

Where the fuck are you?

Nowhere!

I asked you before also… remember?

Sometimes I feel that the bible bullshits about the day Jesus will return, and the day it'll all be sorted out. It even warns us of scoffers who are not patient with God.

I often wonder how can anyone be patient when they hear the screams of children with limbs blown off, running around 'Mariupol' and 'Kharkiv' while that sick evil bastard Putin lives in his compound and denies he's doing anything wrong?

And people say that people with my condition are sick! We have confusion and anxiety due to a brain disease; nothing like that evil bastard.

If I was the head of NATO, I'd have called Putin's bluff and I'd have gone in to Russia and I'd have taken the sick bastard out. If I got my hands on that evilness; I'd do something better, definitely better for sure.

So, Mark Noble has something he can look back on, and I'm very happy for him because he's a good guy and he was a damn good footballer – but not a patch on Steven Gerrard!

So these people have been lucky; and people tell me not to look back, with more than half my fucking life ruined. And when I meet women, they look at me like I'm some kind of an alien. I can't meet anyone for shit and at this stage, I don't care because some women will give you attention if you give them enough money…

I used to think it was about looks and sometimes love but half of both genders have no interest in that. Look at pornography; gorgeous young girls are wasting their beauty in doing ugly things..

And then you try to turn to God for some kind of solace. And he is nowhere to be found… or was I not looking hard enough?

And then it's all about competing now among the young; who are all competing for jobs. They don't trust each other.

When I was in college, the students were all friends and trusted each other and drank together and had fun.

Nowadays the guys put Rohypnol in the girls' drinks and rape them. And the 17-year-old girls have fucking sugar Daddies as opposed to working four nights a week in a Dublin restaurant for €200 - because some sick bastard *(her landlord)* is so cruel and fucking selfish that he charges the college students €400 a week to stay in his shithole of an apartment.

Why is everybody so horrible to each other?

I'm not saying that I'm the most stunning looking person but what I know is that I'm the kindest person and yet nobody wants me; and there are absolute bastards out there who girls chase and get used and hurt by and they're so stupid and they go back for more. Youth is so wasted on the young!

Most of the under 30's may be articulate and educated, but they are immoral people, with millions of euros on them. And then, you have all the arseholes in their forties who have big jobs and have no regards for their wives and the marriage is over once the kids start secondary school.

At least I cry out to God. And I used to try and live by a moral code.

But I've given up now. I go to sex workers because I can't meet someone permanent.

I have happy times with kind friends but not with female friends. Every time I think I've met a nice woman on the internet, she turns out to be a scammer. Nobody trusts anyone anymore. Therefore, why not just go with the flow! And hopefully, this fucked-up world will end; if Jesus will ever return. Because it's a beautiful world. But the only horrible thing is that the beauty is confined to 70% of the population.

If we could just weed out the selfish, nasty people and let the rest of us enjoy our lives in this world in peace, then people who are liars, hypocrites, greedy and selfish – politicians, the rock stars, film stars, TV personalities, the registrars, money grabbers, and not to forget the corrupt business people will have nowhere to exist…

The same to be done in all countries. Weed out the sewage and eliminate them, those who do not have a kind heart, which I think is more than two third of the people. And only leave the lovely, kind, and caring people on the planet earth…

Sadly, it won't happen. Thankfully, this life ends. And I used to believe in eternal life!

I think now that – there's just more bullshit to be spread around like a politician's promise.

Scammers

There are plenty of male scammers out there but there are also more than a fair share of female scammers all the same.

Everyone goes on about the fact that it's hard to meet someone nowadays and a lot of people are trying to get revenge on each other; making this world an even worse place to live in. Men who have experienced a bad marriage just want sex and women want sex and revenge at the same time!

Let me tell you about the two Russian bitches who tried to scam me. Here's what the first one texted me after our initial conversation. Natalya was her name.

'Hi Richard, it was so good to receive your email yesterday and to hear about your life in Ireland. I am 45 years old and I am divorced. I have one son who is in boarding school – 200 miles from our home.'

(This 'one child ruse' is a regular ploy).

She went on…

'He is twelve years of age and is in the first year in a boarding school one hundred miles from Moscow, about 70 miles from me.'

'I work here in Russia as an office administrator for a medical practice.'

(Bullshit!! She's probably a cleaner).

'My Mother died last year *(lie)* and I have nothing to keep me here in Russia, however, now I've met a lovely man like you and you speak so kindly to me, you and are such a gentleman. I simply love your photograph. I keep it by my bedside every night and you are the first person I see when I wake up each day.'

Now comes the real thing…

'I am trying to save the money to come to your country but I also have to pay the fees for my son Alex's education. I will try to come to you by mid-April. I long to be with you. You know you can trust me Richard, so would you be able to send me six hundred euros so I can book now for Dublin and I will have saved up the money, which I will give you when we meet in three months? Just so as I can be sure of getting to you as soon as possible… I can't wait to be with you! Lots of love Richard. Natalya..... '

'Yeah yeah yeah you're so genuine lovely *(Bitch)* Natalya. I know you drive so get into your car, rev up and fuck off, you sick scam artist bitch...

And women give out about men???!!!

The number of bitches online is astounding.

I Think I Know

Why My Prayers are Not Answered

Honest to God we all pray for things in this part of the world that we feel we should have. More money, for example – and better cars, bigger houses... the list is endless …

What I wonder and thus far fail to understand; is why has the world become so worldly? *Or has it always been like this?* Maybe I have an answer to that in between those 5 minutes of freedom, when I can feel good, when I am not delusional, when I can enjoy moments as I know the clock is ticking before he, my friend *(delusion)* returns...

Who said? "health is Wealth"?

I am so grateful to the American philosopher Ralph Waldo Emerson who first coined this term, 'health is wealth' in 1860. And yet, most of us knowingly ignore the fact and continue taking life for granted. Pause! We forget the simplest things, especially the 'normal' people but what they should do really is to ask us the value of those simplest things, like taking a walk in the park to casual and happy conversations with friends to looking at the sun and the birds without feeling the anxiety and delusions and the misery. Look at us! If you still don't get it, then ask yourselves! If that doesn't work either, then come and live with us just for a day! And then you'll know…

We look at millionaires and sigh about our wage packets and our bills, while half the world lives on a handful of rice and lentils a day. And water carried for miles by women just to feed their offspring enough food so that hopefully they are alive tomorrow.

Have we any fucking idea at all?

And we go out for a meal and splash out on big fancy meals and luxurious desserts with wine and champagne and roasted coffee and then we give €5.00 to Africa and maybe another €2.00 to Afghanistan. We really don't think.

And I am one of the worst culprits in the world. I prayed a couple of times to meet a girlfriend but I never persisted and then I watched porn in anger and went on a spree of having sex with sex workers. I did feel it would take time to find a woman but I didn't stick with it. Instead, I flew into a rage in the face of

God like I do regularly, and I spent five grand on the sex workers.

The Three Pulls

I have never taken a street drug in my life... with the exception of the famous three pulls *(of hash)*! "Three Pulls," my nickname in Glory Hall.

I remember when Nick Hayes and Paul, standing at the door of the Glory Hall on a windy March morning in 1989, chitchatting. It was a fine Friday morning.

"Anything interesting happening today Paul"? Asked Hayes with a curious but untroubled look, as he puckered to take a drag of his cigarette.

Paul shook his head and sighed, "Nah Nick! Not much."

"But the doctors will be here later… oh hang on Bill!" Hayes exclaimed, "isn't Rich in today?".

After a moment of silence, Paul took a fleeting sigh and whispered, "think so." "And Dr. Tom Smith is coming too!" *(The doctor).*

"We'll have a ball. Rich will be chasing them around the place asking about his delusion - it'll be a pantomime!!"

"Oh yeah…" said Paul.

Vinny heard them, "ah, poor Rich."

"Yes…" said Hayes, "God help him. it's sad but it's fucking hilarious and we'll be in stitches laughing."

***

I arrived twenty minutes later carrying the tremendous misery of delusion *(my normal).* I recall praying the doctors would talk to me as they had spoken to me last week.

The truth is… I needed constant assurance, looking for some kind of closure on my delusions and ultimately feel some peace.

They arrived four hours beyond lunch time. After enduring a tough and insane morning, sorting the black bags, I was trying to concentrate on what I was doing for the long morning.

The delusion would temporarily leave me for a few minutes but will come back again for at least an hour before it'd take a few minutes off.

I can't recall when was the last time I did get a bit of craic as my closest comrade *(delusion)* always wanted my best attention.

"But doctor Smith," I would say *(at lunchtime)*; "are you sure the three pulls wouldn't destroy the brain?"

"No Richard, they wouldn't, your system has ways of getting rid of the tiny amounts of poison and as a matter of fact it has left your system years ago, I repeat - all gone!"

The doctor broke the news of hope. "Yes Richard, it's all gone."

"But how many brain cells did I kill Doc with the three pulls of hash?" I couldn't believe it.

"None Richard!" Tom spoke, "you didn't smoke enough."

"But if it hit my brain, then I'm in trouble – isn't that right? So, do not try to fool me doctor. If it went up to my brain, then there's damage and I know it doc – I know it." I was insistent.

"That's nonsense Richard. There's no damage, you're absolutely fine. It's all disappeared Richard, it's all gone!" Tom seemed certain.

The reassurance from Tom awakened a thousand hopes in my mind…

One day I might see the light…

The doctors were hopeful. I guess this *'hope'* sank so deep in me that it kept me going till date… but I am still dependent on the pills and it has been almost 35 years!

Not a joke, not even close!

But then again what else could they do? They had already told me all they could. The doctors had been very understanding. What more could I ask for? I am gratified…

I never gave up on the idea that one day the hope would turn into reality…

I just hope that it's not the end...

I know how unwell I was and also saddled with this thought, but the good news was… there was hope that it would ease in time; if I exercised and took my medication, stayed sensible and ate properly.

Guess what?

Hope is an amazing thing... it keeps you going!

As Martin Luther King (Jr) rightly said with poise in his heart:

"We must accept finite disappointment, but never lose infinite hope."

– Martin Luther King, Jr.

For me, it meant that my unsolicited friend *(delusion)* would stop interfering with my beautiful brain's cells and it would all ease in time; provided I remained active and religiously took my pills.

You won't believe it but I also learnt that one can essentially fight for sensibility, it's all in the mind.

Therefore, if I stayed sensible and ate properly, I could get rid of my very old friend or at the least have some time alone. I could sense it was time I did!

"At times, our own light goes out and is rekindled by a spark from another person. Each of us has cause to think with deep gratitude of those who have lighted the flame within us."

– Albert Schweitzer

***

My real drug problem had to do with the tons of medication that I had to consume.

The question is why on earth do we have to stomach all these drugs that only stone you to death or even make you feel like the lamb taken for slaughter?

But then, there were no two ways about it.

I had to endure the medication and continue to battle on. At least now I was out of the hospital and at best I could go up to Glory Hall, try and interact with people and be in 'regular' company. Then who knows - perhaps even initiate the journey of hope - being healthy; but I also knew that it would take a long time.

First step is the hardest but that's all it takes.

For me, the goalmouth was getting back to normal and being mentally well and that wouldn't happen overnight.

This required Willpower and Patience apart from the Medication and diet.

Times had progressed and Researches have enhanced the possibility of fresh neurons in an old brain being developed…

The doctors never really tell you exactly how many years you'll suffer for, how long will you be ill for, or perhaps they themselves don't know! I presume, they are just not supposed to say.

Doctors know that half the people who are ill, recognized that it could take up to fifteen years to recuperate. This very thought was enough to make someone jump out the window or into the river.

Don't believe the thought never occurred in my mind!

Like I implied earlier, the suicide attempts are quite common amongst schizophrenia patients. Let's just say only 20-40% do not take this step.

Do the math, imagine the dilemma of the people with mental health struggles.

In addition, those who don't have a harder challenge must relish what they have; because life for us is just not the reflection of what *'perfectly fine'* people know of.

The Classified Idiots

The doctors would admit you into the hospital and tell you that they were just taking you in for some tests; but you'd end up rotting in the ward with dozens of other sufferers.

The specialists won't even bother with giving you any feedback - and all this would go on for no less than two months; until you reach the edge and yell at the top of your voice for them to communicate the information or at least update us regarding the required facts.

Bloody doctors!

Besides, if you were going fine on your medication, nothing would be changed for months – just because they don't want to rock the boat and as a consequence, you'd be going around like a fucking zombie, barely able to get out of bed until 3 'o clock in the afternoon whereas the medics would be encouraging you to try and acquire some work!!

My mind often wondered – why don't those bastards take the drugs themselves for a week or two and see just how fuckin' enthusiastic they would feel working with this kind of debility, not helped by the amount of shit that they prescribe us; and refuse to reduce it for years and years and years.

They "the classified idiots" deserve to have a taste of their own medicine!

I can categorically relate to this Quote by **Courtney C. Stevens**:

"Nothing changes, IF nothing changes!"

If I'm absolutely candid, I used to go to bed with the intention of getting up at 8.30am and going to my course or Glory Hall *(at the time)* or wherever I was attending. Even if I was out of bed by 11.30am, I'd be doing just fine. It would be no less than an achievement!

Hero Worshipping Idiots

“What’s wrong with society, Paul?” I said to him at the doorway of GH.

“Dunno,” he said, pulling on his fag on this wet, windy, Tuesday morning in early April.

The big oak tree on the lawn swayed violently in the strong winds. Paul and I grinned as Mark O’Casey arrived in to Bailey Hall walking one step forward and two steps back.

“Part of his illness.” I said as Paul nodded.

Back to our conversation:

“The fucking war in Syria and now Covid and on top of it that evil dirt bag Putin attacks Ukraine! I said two days earlier as he moved his tanks in and started bombing. Innocent people’s lives would now be destroyed. I’d give as much money as I could but that’d be a few hundred euros at best.”

"Ah the world's fucked, Rich, and everyone knows it. But people don't want to sound negative. There are still a lot of positive things happening, nevertheless there is some terrible shit going on." Paul tried to stay positive.

"At least Liverpool won at the weekend', I said, "and Chelsea lost to Spurs." I chuckled to Paul's annoyance being a staunch Chelsea fan.

I said, "when you think about all the unsung heroes in this country and then you have some morons in MONTROSE. Not 'some' but quite a few, interviewing the shitty and X Factor boy bands. The death of proper music, with thousands of really good bands out there trying to get a record deal and then you have these idiots extorting money out of the innocent young girls who'll very soon realise what a load of shit they are. And the whole regiment of idiots who work for X factor; except for Louis Walsh - who has pedigree. Trying to turn idiots into musicians and then they actually think they have succeeded!!"

"Eh! I know." Paul breathed out as he took the last drag of his cigarette.

"As I was saying Paul; thousands of bands, really good bands who put blood, sweat and tears into their demonstrations and EP's while the X factor shit makes money for the gobshites that are in these bands."

"What fuckin bands?" Brian asked.

"I know, Paul. They just stand on stage and swing their groins back and forth while all the girls scream; and these morons actually think that they have talent. There's no justice here and that lanky matchstick on the Late Show, grovelling to the celebrities, while he earns €750,000 *(or so did before the pandemic).* Montrose - our national broadcaster, a shower of clowns." I was so pissed.

"I emailed in for five years trying to get an interview on mental health. I never ever got a single reply. I'd love to burn the entire place down Paul." I was feeling tremendously angry.

"God Rich, take your tablets." Paul expressed concern, thinking it's the schizophrenia speaking.

"I will…" I said, "because if there's a shortage of Olanzapine, the place will go up in flames. Shower of wankers that they are."

"You really don't like them, do you?" Paul said. "Let's go inside. The misty rain is soaking me."

I went inside with Paul and we went up to the computers. This haunted old house of people with mental illness complemented the sickness we all had. It was dark and sombre, and had a calm ambience about it, however it would certainly depress you enough…

The walls to the staircase were yellow and the walls upstairs were yellow too and the office door was painted cream, white and pale blue. Many days I chased the doctor around this building, trying to ascertain how badly damaged my brain was from the three pulls of hash.

'Schizophrenia' is a darkness that won't let you see the sun even when you're outside breathing it. You are locked into a terrifying existence, where 'well' people will say, you just need to cheer up and have a pint…

The reality is; psychosis takes years to pull out of, and we live in a different world than that of people who are not ill.

Beauty Dies

Marie

She was only 22. And so beautiful…

Long, flowing, blond hair, with flushed pink cheeks on a stunningly well-proportioned young face.

The reason her face was flushed pink was due to anxiety.

She tried hard to smile and be spontaneous.

What was really difficult for her was the fact that she attracted so much male attention that she just even didn't need, at least not so much!

'Marie' wasn't well.

She grew to trust a guy called David.

David was a good guy who had no ulterior motive. What mattered to him was just her sanity, her peace of mind and any happiness that he could bring her and make her feel it deep in her heart. It was truly all that he wanted.

He told the other guys in the day centre to leave her in peace.

Most of them had enough cop-on to leave her alone, but the centre wasn't only just catering for the mentally ill, there were dysfunctional juveniles' youth *(mainly teenage boys)* on the campus also and most of them were totally sex starved.

It was very stressful for poor Marie. She only trusted David.

He had befriended her the first week she was there and she just felt she could trust him. He spoke to her just like two people would normally chat. He was in his twenties and more mature than the other clowns who desperately kept trying to impress her with their childish behaviour. But that's teenage boys – infatuated, idiotic, immature, lacking any insight into people's feelings and having little or no idea how the world works.

Maria had spoken to her doctor the week before.

She felt the centre had helped her get back into a structure, but she told the doctor her anxiety levels were high because of the male – female ratio which was three to one, and she and Sandra Brady were the two girls the lads leered at all day, whispering dirty words to each other about the two ladies.

"I really want to leave and do a community employment scheme" she said as calmly as possible to the doctor…

"Because I would like to go to college and study horticulture so I could get a Gardening Community Employment Scheme."

The patronising wanker looked at her and cut her short saying, she wasn't well enough yet and that he felt another year at the centre would help her.

"Not until you're ready for the real world," said the patronising bastard.

She knew she couldn't get emotional or that would only prolong her stay doing catering in this shithole and her stupid and naive parents had agreed to do exactly as the doctors said.

"Because they know best," her bogshite farmer father said.

(They know best – My arse!)

The quack wouldn't even give her a sleeper as she was having trouble sleeping with the thoughts of having to attend this dump every day to be leered at and approached by the ugly cigarette smoking teenage arseholes, who couldn't string a sentence together but wanted to kiss her.

Off went the quack, the young know-all trainee psychiatrist, *(€130,000 a year wasted on his salary),* driving his Lexus, on to meet his next unfortunate victim.

***

Marie was found dead three days later…

She set herself on fire in the ladies' room. She poured the cooking oil from the kitchen onto her apron and set herself on fire.

Imagine, what could be going in a human being's mind that it would send such extreme signals, and more so, such a miserable way of taking one's own life!

Trust me when I say, I know the feeling!

The wanker of a young psychiatrist didn't even hear about it for three weeks and when he did, it barely raised his pulse pressure. He just didn't bother!

Fact is, the majority of psychiatrists are assholes.

Till Death do us Part

The beautiful Annie

"Richard let's get out of here." Annie said.

Paul Kelly was staring at her again and it was making her agitated and uncomfortable.

"Let's go over to Stillorgan for a coffee and a chat." I said.

I was visiting Annie in the hospital and she had her clothes back and was out of the lock up ward. Luckily she was quite well again and had permission to go to Stillorgan. I was dying to get out of the place so we could go over to the wall and have a long kiss. Her kiss was heavenly and I was thrilled I had taken the courage to ask her out and she had said 'yes.' She was stunningly beautiful but badly affected by mental illness. She had paranoia and delusions and heard voices but she wouldn't admit she had schizophrenia. She was simply not able to accept it. We all knew she had it and I was trying very hard to be kind to her. I decided to never challenge her on this point as I knew how she felt and how it's often too hard to accept.

"That bastard Kelly was staring at me again Richard!!"

"Why don't you sort him out Rich??"

"Ah God Annie..." I said, "you hardly want me to beat him up over staring at you, he's ill and he's sex starved. I can't harm him; goodness knows his life is hard enough as it is. Anyway be reasonable Annie. I'm not the jealous type.

"Well talk to him then," she said.

"I'll ask him not to stare at you." I said, "and that it makes you uncomfortable but let's face it Annie, you're the best bit of scenery in that depressing ward; full of ill people. Kelly is only human!."

***

I went out with Annie when I was 27 and after a few months, we had sex and boy, it was beautiful!

I was worried that with the sex, I had taken advantage of her, but she assured me that I hadn't and for many years after she became unwell, I minded her.

She was beautiful, her body was heavenly and so was her kiss. The surprising element was that she also had schizophrenia – but wasn't really willing to face it. She was in high demand, hence would continuously deny the fact that she had mental illness. She was extremely paranoid, nonetheless I liked her. She thought she'd marry one day, whereas I knew I wouldn't. We went our separate ways mercifully. Her mental health continued to deteriorate so much so, that ten years later she took her own life.

***

It is so very sad, yet people simply don't give a shit. They laugh at the mentally ill because it's so *'uncool'* to have mental illness.

People think they are superior because they don't suffer with the paranoia, the anxiety and delusions. They have no idea what the feeling is like… until one or two of these fucking arseholes smoke hash every day for a couple of years, ending up with psychosis and several physical ailments.

Fucking morons, pure idiots!

It's been ten years! Annie passed on ten years ago – I fail to understand how can years fly so fast when a day in my life has only been dawdling. As it seemed, time went by at an altitude of 90000 feet, leaving me behind with no choice except to contend with my shadows.

Annie was the only way I could muster up any positivity; instead of by pumping myself up with tons and tons of antidepressants, thus deceiving my mind, trying to enjoy the false highs.

Understanding Women

I wonder if this would come as a surprise to you that I was awfully sex starved and tremendously disillusioned with my efforts in vain to meet someone.

It simply wasn't going to happen.

The fainthearted never win the fair ladies and I was no different. I had zero confidence!

It's comprehensible that since I had been on medication for over 20 years now, trying to deal with this horrifying sickness; girls typically looked at me with disdain. It was probably because my self-esteem was so low. I was totally sex deprived.

Truth be told, I hadn't touched a girl since Annie.

I went to 'Kate' for counselling. She was very kind to me. She heard me…

Since I hadn't kissed a girl for twelve years or hugged a woman for the same amount of time, I was frustrated. Perhaps it was for that reason that I was overweight, constantly banged up to the eyes on antipsychotics and incapable of talking to women. I can't really say…

Women – they can be so fucking patronising when you try to make their acquaintance.

If the ladies think you're trying to chat them up, they try to slag you off – and then loads of girls wonder why they have no boyfriend!

Nowadays you see them going into town, all dressed up, *(sometimes half naked although that's their entitlement)* waiting with their slick dress, charm and a bottle of Rohypnol and MDMA; but the slick sly smooth talkers who'll chat them up, use them, rape them, and perchance kill them…

Many nice girls from various countries have been trafficked into the sex industry by these evil bastards. While poor schizophrenic Richard (me) or some very decent friends as well are often unable to even meet someone.

Typically, the good find the good eventually, but it's hard for people with schizophrenia.

The Pain of the Hardman

The Invisible Wanderers of Dublin

You see him leaning against the wall smoking his fags and chewing his gum and tattooed to bits *(although I like a couple of them)* covered from head to toe in this art-like appeal to humanity to care about him and his girlfriend, his kid, his siblings and all the people on gear in his neighbourhood, and all those who died because of it.

They're all on gear because people don't give a shit.

Yes, socialism doesn't always work as some people work much harder than others and maybe he spurned a few good chances to get on - but if you knew his family set up, with an alcoholic, violent father and a sedative induced pill swallowing mother, who can't get through the day without six Valium's and six Xanax's... as she had also witnessed the violence that comes with the drug dealing as part of a gang.

These people only take drugs to numb the pain – pain of the past, pain of today and the pain they know they'll have to face in the future.

The guy in Blackrock drives his Mercedes to work and puts in 20 cents for these people on the plate and then brings his family out for a slap-up meal in the Westbury and is glad he prayed for all his family.

This wanker actually thinks he's a good guy!

Get out your wallet you bollox and put €50 on the plate for poorer people. We're all very good at giving to foreign charities but what about the social drug migrants of Dublin who wander our streets stoned, in mental agony?

Nobody cares, people just walk by them making sure they don't make eye contact with these poor people. There are a lot of bastards in Dublin and I'm not talking about the hardmen.

Will You Strike Me Down Jesus?

Trust me when I say, these antidepressants can make a person feel a lot better! But then again, you talk at hundred miles an hour and most of it is rubbish.

If only someone could read the inside of our minds – especially the part where the loyal friend 'delusion' dwells! If that was reality, then gratitude would be the theme of this earth full of normal people!

Having said that, I watched a lot of people die – even those also who took their medication right!

Rest assured, I told my registrars *(doctors)* that if they didn't want another statistic, I would do whatever I needed to do in order to stay alive. And that meant occasionally devouring antidepressants to live through the dark periods.

I know that from the outside, it simply appears to be self-deceit. I was quite mindful about it myself. At times, guilt got the best of me in terms of being reliant on a provisional resolution, a short-cut. Maybe I was being a coward, maybe I did not have the courage to face it, to go through the storm and end up on the other side with a permanent rainbow waiting. Well, perhaps not permanent!

After all, Nothing in life has permanence; right?

***

I felt suicidal on and off for years. Constantly persecuted by delusions, going into churches and getting down on my knees and begging God for help.

I suppose the reason He didn't help much was because I didn't persevere, my relationship with God was kind one day and the other day, I would curse and complain and that is all due to the mood swings, thanks to my schizophrenia!

I often talked to God and asked HIM to pardon me or at least understand my problem.

When nobody understands, God does!

To this day, I wonder if I would be received by the fires of hell when I die. I spoke to a priest and also to my amazing counsellor. I also felt that my prayers were heard. I sensed that God has responded to my quandary like an echo in my mind…

'If you persist for years with prostitutes, then I'll punish you, whereas right now I forgive you but you must change eventually'

Yes Jesus, absolutely! I will do my damndest to break the chains over the next couple of years. I really intend to because some of my friends think it's okay but at the same time, a few Christian friends have cautioned me.

"But Kevin!!" I said. "Look at this horror war in Ukraine and I do believe Jesus exists but why does he allow these terrible things to happen and not intervene?"

"I have suffered in my life." I continued, "but it's nothing compared to what this sick bastard Putin is doing to the Ukrainian people. I genuinely feel that NATO should have gone in initially and taken him out."

"I met people in the hospital who are sick but they all told me they were not as sick as Putin is. He's the scum of the earth. He's the genital wart on the balls of humanity!!"

"And where is God?? And why the hell won't he intervene??!!" I was burning with pain…

"I know Rich." Kevin said with a sigh.

"But Jesus said that things would come to justice on the last day. And during the last days and the rapture of this world; justice will prevail."

"It's a fallen world Rich." Kevin continued his efforts to calm my nerves. "Do you expect God to go around sorting out every problem and healing everyone?? That's not his way!"

"I know Kevin." I said. "I'm very childish when it comes to God. I feel you can lean on him for everything."

"Well, for one thing Rich, He said you don't persevere in prayer and you have to do that!!" Kevin exclaimed.

"I've also committed bad sins and often I didn't repent. I tell God I'll repent later. I know you can sometimes fool humans but you can never fool God. He knows and understands more than you think." He spoke with such honesty that it clearly seemed he really meant it.

"Well, I've gone to hookers because of being sex starved and I know this displeases God. But it's a dilemma as I couldn't meet anyone for years. I don't know what to do as I have needs too and a lot of mentally ill people commit suicide, one of the big reason being, they are sex starved."

I was in the church praying. I felt that I needed to talk to God, and repent. I looked up at the crucifix on the altar:

I said…

"Dear God," I went for sex today. I really enjoyed it, although I have to pay for it. If you are going to strike me down for this, I understand. I don't know if you are annoyed with me, because I don't know if you hear my prayers. Sometimes, I can feel your compassion, and you have done wonderful things for some people. I ask you now – if you can't forgive me – to please try to understand."

On the way out of the church, I blessed myself, kneeled and left respectfully.

I felt lighter saying this out loud like a confession!

And I hope Jesus won't strike me down…

Somebody was Kind

Threshold

It all started at the counselling where I told my counsellor 'Kate' that I went from the age of 27 to 39 without even holding a girl's hand, let alone kissing one or having a hug. I suddenly felt a rage inside me. I had witnessed all my friends getting married and leading very 'normal' lives *(i.e. whatever normal is for us suffering).*

I wrote my first little book "The Mood Swings". When I went down to Naas to launch it, all my mates were there with their wives talking about their kids and I looked around and repeatedly asked myself, 'why me?' What had I done to deserve 25 years of suffering and all of them had hardly suffered a day in their lives. I know some people suffer even more than me but very few in Ireland. I had hardly had a day's peace for 25 years.

Every day was dogged by delusions and anxiety and depression. Battling hard to try and go on, to battle for survival, to do my best to cope. You think when you get this illness, that you'll be back on life's treadmill a year or so later and that you'll catch up with your friends; hoping in vain!

It took me one year to become totally psychotic and ill and has taken me over 30 years to recover. But I'll have to take medication for the rest of my life. Although I now feel blessed indeed.

I went to loads of escorts for sex and shortly, here is where I'll tell my story about it…

I'm not proud of it and lots of women will vilify me but then again when you pray about it and pray for years and years to meet someone but girls only stare at you with disdain *(because I'm somewhat overweight due to medication)* and I don't have qualifications and I wasn't able to be relaxed or spontaneous and it was fairly obvious I was on medication as I looked exhausted half the time and my self-esteem was like most people with mental illness *(at rock bottom).*

I didn't know how to boost my self-worth since people are not stupid and I'm sure they could tell I was sick. And the way it is with schizophrenia, the ill remains ill and the well remains well and that's life, that's the fact of life!

Hence there I was with my extremely kind and attractive lady counsellor and I suddenly grabbed my groin, stood up and said, “I have had it. I’m never going to meet anyone. Nobody is interested. I have money, I have savings, I’m going to fuck as many escorts in Dublin as I can.”

Kate was so calm, she wasn’t even upset. She wasn’t offended *(whereas in my heart, I felt disrespectful to her).* Instead, she calmly spoke, “go and have sex, nobody can judge you Richard, it’s your decision, you have an illness.”

To this day, she has been so kind and has supported me and stood by me, and I adore her for her kindness.

The Debacle

Call Girls & The Cops

And so my escapade began. I went online and checked out *escortsireland.com.* I found it amazing - just how hot and sexy the escorts were as I read through their profiles. Most of them said they loved sex and really enjoyed what they do. I wondered. I felt for them. I found it even sad that they had to have sex for money, but at best least Irish men are renowned for being gentle with them and any of the girls I visited told me they felt safe and were not worried about their security and would only focus on making money. And they were well paid.

When I went to any girl, I would at first apologise profusely for coming, which they couldn't believe; and I'd always pay them at least €100 more than they asked for. I felt so unattractive to women that I used to ask them if they could actually go through with it? I felt it'd probably be hell for the girl or girls *(I went to two sometimes)*.

God bless the poor women - they will have sex with you if you pay them money. They need to pay their rents plus pay for travel and food. It's also a dodgy business as girls can be attacked, but at least most of the time in Ireland, the girls are safer than they are elsewhere on the continent.

The first day I went I was nervous, very nervous. Two years before this, I'd had a girlfriend who was a sufferer but we had gone our separate ways and I now had developed erectile dysfunction. I told my G.P. about it.

"It's the medication." he said. I had assumed as much. I remember now a dialogue with a frustrated girlfriend of mine:

"I can't maintain my hard-on. Sorry."

"Oh try, I really want you to ride me."

"I think it's the meds (medication)."

"I'll give you head instead."

"I am really sorry, love, I hate leaving you unsatisfied. I'll go to my GP and get some Viagra."

"That'll be great, so as soon as you get them, call me."

"Byyyeeee."

Years later, I was able to manage it because at this point, he gave me Viagra and on the internet, I had read about things that are helpful such as coffee and ginseng. Also, red wine and other stuff like spinach and magnesium *(spinach contains magnesium).*

Hence, I was ready to fuck and I was filled with lust!

I was going to get the two gorgeous young German girls, who had reassured me that they'd give me anything I wanted for the money. They said they'd charge me a total sum of €500 for two hours with them.

"What door number are you, girls? And which apartment?"

"Come into the courtyard and take the first turn on the right, go around that corner and it is the second door on the left. Apartment no 5. Ring the bell and I will let you in."

Actually, the build-up to these sessions was nearly as exciting as the act itself; the expectation; the journey to the destination; getting lost; a second and a third call to the girls – where are you? – the fear that there might be a pimp or that she might be aggressive;

or that she keeps the money and tells me to fuck off or she will call the police.

And then … and then … and … omg…

The door opens.
The holy grail.
I have found what I am looking for.
Legs;
Suspenders;
Tights;
Thong in vagina;
Black straps;
High heels …
Oh my goddddddddddddd.

I always check the bottle of wine and the glass they give me in case they are dodgy and spike the alcohol. Nobody does, to be fair as a rule.

I had an incredible time. I profusely apologised though as I sat with the two of them on the bed before we started. I begged them to get out of this business before they got hurt or damaged and I gave them an extra €100.

'We just want to have sex with you.'

'Ohh, nice one.'

So, one of the girls removed what she had to.

Finally, we got down to a very enjoyable two hours out of this world!! Man, I was on cloud 9, on top of the moon and far away from this planet… I guess…

Three weeks later I was craving more… I rang one of the girls again and she said she had a new partner and that they had moved to Sandyford. However, she also said she'd love to see me again.

That Saturday afternoon with all my medications taken including the two tablets of Viagra; I headed up to Sandyford. I had no idea that the new girl had had trouble getting into Ireland and had slipped through security on a dodgy passport.

I met them and wanted to French kiss them as well as everything else.

"Do you French kiss?"

"Oh nooo. That's €50 extra each." (They won't be getting a fucking tip).

"Ahh come onnnn, that is very expensive. A French kiss goes with sex."

"It is not always nice."

"I cleaned my teeth four times and I have a packet of mints."

They laughed and thought that was funny. €100 later, and my tongue was like a fish in the river Shannon.

And so I had to pay an extra €50 each. It cost me a fortune. €600 for 90 minutes with the two of them.

I was anxious hence did a lot of talking. It was in fact *the Lexapro* talking! I was on Lexapro and that makes one excessively chatty. But the sex was great and so was the French kissing. I was certainly in heaven...

A big sack of condoms was just about visible in the drawer beside the bed. Now another issue with Lexapro is that it takes you longer to come. However, after about an hour and 20 minutes, I was fucking the smaller one while the other one enjoyed a cup of tea. I was waiting for 'Agatha' *(the taller one)* to come back in for the 4th of July finish.

As I was just about to climax, there was a violent rapping at the door. 'Sally' *(the shorter one)* jumped off me and put on a dressing gown. I was lying there with a horn like a Wavin pipe on me. I just thought it was a neighbour of theirs or perhaps a wrong number. The next thing I heard was, "this is the police, open the door."

They would have broken the door down if Agatha hadn't answered it. The cops burst in – there were three of them including a female officer. I dived off the bed still with a large shaft on me. The cops addressed me, "right, you're being summoned to court for having sex with two prostitutes illegally for money."

I asked if I would go to prison and they said "no you'll be fined after a court appearance."

They asked me what was in my bag. But all I had in there were just a few books – Horticulture books and a novel to be precise. They were satisfied with that after checking and then the female officer told me she wanted to talk to me.

'Shit!' I thought, I have to get the horn to go down or I'll get in more trouble. I had been just about to ejaculate when they burst in. I thought about going into the toilet and finishing myself off but it'd take too long. She wanted to talk to me in two minutes, that is exactly what she said.

I had to get to the bathroom and pour cold water on the bloody horn. It was still throbbing and bigger than a normal six and a half inches. I tried to get it into my trousers and push it to the side, else it'd be obvious and could possibly stick up into her. Gosh; how disrespectful!

"Get down ye bastard," I said as I poured cold water on it.

"Will you be long?" She said. "I'm very busy."

"I'll be with you in a minute!" I said desperately as I poured yet another glass of cold water on it. (Thankfully there was a glass in the bathroom).

About three minutes later, with the horn now floored; (although still about four inches long) I came out of the bathroom meekly and told the female guard that I was ready to talk to her. She asked me what had taken me so long in the bathroom? She knew the truth. I wondered if she wanted a cheap thrill? And yet, I had to verbally state the reality.

"I'm very sorry" I said, "I was trying to get my erection down."

She didn't flinch.

"I don't mean to be disrespectful," I said, "but you asked."

"I know." She smiled.

And then started the real interrogation...

"So you had full sex?" She questioned. *Wasn't it obvious?* I felt like saying…

"Well you hardly think we were playing tiddly winks, yes." I answered.

"With both girls? She asked.

"Yes" I said…*(are you stupid or what?)*

"And is this the first time you have used the services of sex workers?" She continued.

"Yes." I lied. *(no, I fuck whenever I feel like it).*

Actually it was only my second time and I intended to have lots and lots more sex. I had schizophrenia and I couldn't meet anyone and I was angry.

The police told me to have no contact with the girls again, and to dress and leave.

Don't ever go to a prostitute again!

The Court Case

It was serious, there was no doubt about it and there was no messing about it. I'd been caught by the police having sex with two sex workers. There was a chance I could be put on the sex offenders' register.

It's so unfair. I've tried to meet somebody and I try to be nice to girls but the agony of being lonely probably shows deeply on my face.

"What am I supposed to do?" I asked a friend.

"I know," he replied. "It's difficult but you could be on the sex offenders' list."

Here I was after 30 years of incessant suffering and mental agony and I had tried so hard to fit into society and here's my friend, who doesn't even believe in God, has lovely, healthy kids and his wife is well and yet he doesn't have any gratitude toward the Almighty for all the blessings he has, and still has to this day.

The solicitor laughed at the police report that said all I did was talk to the girls and hardly got down to any sex. Actually, I was so much under the influence of anti-depressants, that I was talking like a mad thing. They told me to "shut up and fuck."

The judge read my doctor's report where I admitted to the crime. I wasn't able to meet anyone and I felt huge pain watching couples with their kids and people getting married *(all of which seems to be the normal route),* while the mentally ill never get well enough to have real families.

Then you have the total idiots going to nightclubs and taking ecstasy and loads of hash and ending up with enduring mental illness. I never did drugs and despite that, I developed schizophrenia. The solicitor knew I'd been to loads of hookers and she was laughing as we left the court.

If the judge only knew what would I be doing to celebrate getting off… I've a nice blonde lined up.

The Fire

With schizophrenia, you lose the years to forge intimate relationships, to fall in love, to study or even train for a steady career. You are lost and trapped in a world full of hair brained delusions, paranoia and suffering all over – a few different uninvited chemicals working differently in your brain, compared to most people.

Imagine, for that… we are abused, not once taken seriously and treated like idiots by the arrogant, young shrinks and registrars. Registrars, the raw 22-year-old males, with no hair on their balls and women who have not even started ovulating; think they know more than the patients themselves about the patient's illness.

Get this clear, MENTALLY ILL people are MORE intelligent than the average man in the street and much more creative in general. Except, they are far less competent than healthy people, for all the torment they have to live with.

Two weeks had passed since my debacle with the two call girls and the police raid. Therefore, I was a bit apprehensive about going back to them. But I had a lot of sex to catch on to calm down my libido and general horniness. I wanted to give plenty of women a good, hard pounding; because I knew I could have it as I paid for it. This was hugely liberating… I would tell them to strip naked and they would have to – or else I wouldn't pay them. If I paid them enough, I was entitled to have any position or situation I wanted!

By God, this was great…

I had ten grand to blow and spend on sex, and these girls were going to get pounded anyway I wanted.

I arrived up to Sandyford and kept my voice down on the phone. The two girls were available. 'Sally' and 'Andrea'.

One of the girls turned out to be the one of the two that I got caught with by the 'Gardai.' The other one was a sexy, Spanish girl, Sally. She stripped me naked and I didn't have a chance to ask them to… *"get out of this seedy business. It was so dangerous!"* I had tried this the last time we met, but once the girls had their money, they just wanted to fuck – and I just wanted to fuck. Either way, it was just 'Fuck'!

Consequently, they got down on it and then I proceeded with Sally on the bed. She was so mad for it. But as they say; no glove, no love…I took out a condom from my pocket and was ready, hard as a rock. 'Andrea' asked me to do it the doggy style as she leaned against the armchair. I gave her a good pounding for at least six or seven minutes. Phew!

***

My clothes were on the floor in the corner of the room, near a lamp stand about three feet from the armchair. We hadn't copped on that the light was on and at one stage Andrea kicked out in pleasure, knocking the lamp over. She and I were oblivious to the fact that my clothes were catching fire, and the next we heard was a loud shriek… It was Andrea, who moments ago, was watching us in action.

She was screaming, "Fire! Fire!" And we turned around jumping from our very awkward positions only to see the three-foot flames soaring up at us. I instantly grabbed my clothes. Luckily, there was a fire extinguisher, which Andrea managed to quench the fire with. The three of us were hopping around, naked, flapping at the fire and whacking the flames with towels. I couldn't manage to save my underpants from the fire, but Sally managed to grab my sizzling and hissing pants, ran over to a sink and doused them under the tap, hence saving my grace. I would have to walk with nothing on beneath…

Unfortunately, she couldn't save the crotch. Coincidentally, I was wearing clean ones that day, hence no smell of Kentucky Fried Chicken *(to be polite)* wafting around the room.

Whilst the fire was being put out and through all the skipping around, my hard-on was intact *(still erect)*. Thankfully, when we finally managed to put the fire out, Sally gave me a hand job and finished me off with a happy ending. Then, the three of us spent time doctoring up the carpet. Unexpectedly, there was a can of Shake and Vac carpet cleaner in the apartment cupboard. We used it and that did a good job making the carpet burn unnoticeable.

I had to walk home like a commando; *Trousers with no underpants.* Also, I was wearing only one sock as understandably the other one was burnt in the fire. But if you ask me the truth, the crotch, the sock or even the unanticipated fire; nothing was ruffling me a tiny bit. To the contrary, I was smiling throughout my way back home…

The bottom-line: *The Fire in my body was soothed… and that's what mattered!*

Porn for Pain

I got my new Smartphone delivered to my house on a Wednesday and by Friday evening, I had watched about three hours of pornography. We all really know that porn is bad and that if God exists, it's an aberration to him.

When a young woman and a young man are growing up, they don't say *"once I grow up, I'm going to be a porn star."* People's circumstances often dictate what they'll do and often have to do, to cope financially or emotionally.

I hadn't been able to meet a nice woman due to the illness I have. I wasn't very lonely but was lonely enough. I really would have loved the companionship of a girlfriend. Instead, for intimacy, I had to rely on sex workers. I discovered a couple who would be friends with me. I would have sex with them and they would talk to me as recompense. I felt very fortunate that I had enough money to be able to be with them now and again. Most people with disabilities of sorts, wouldn't be able to afford to go to a sex worker, not a chance, ever. It would be easier for you to comprehend this, if you have the slightest idea what we, the mentally unwell people feel. Yes, we have feelings too! Thus, it all had been accordingly reassuring. We mostly have to be content with the alternate of what normal people can effortlessly have.

By now, I was watching violent pornography and was thoroughly liking seeing women being double and triple penetrated. *This is truly dreadful and looking back – I'm truly ashamed of it.* But it was all for the reason that they treated me like shit. To put it more simply, people with schizophrenia are humans too! Or would you believe otherwise?

Sadly, the fact that most of the time men and women don't understand each other leads men to violence against women. I know that this is no excuse, this is no reason, but you just need to sit down with your wife, girlfriend or your partner and indeed listen to them. That's all it takes and that is all that's required. However, mostly men just don't listen.

I hate fighting with women. I dread it. They are quite often right also; but every now and then they get so emotional or verbally vicious that the *fight* becomes unavoidable. But then again, women carry added weight in life. Extra burden in a family situation is frequently encountered by women. They do 70% of the children's nurturing and yet every so often they suffer and feel trapped in marriages that don't work; because the man is selfish.

When a woman gives out to me, I listen intently and try to see my faults like *introspection*, or if I really have any grounds for disputing anything. Her typical opinion is that I have no grounds. Women are generally great people. I wish I could find one to love, really and profoundly cherish for life but with my illness, I don't stand a chance, perhaps one day I will...

India

Hazy but not Crazy

"I'm going to India Mum, I'm going for two weeks."

"Ah Rich, really?" said Mum apprehensively. "Please don't go."

"I'll be fine mum." I said, "I need a break, just for two weeks."

I knew Mum would need me for the rest of her life after this, so I wanted one last experience before I put my shoulder to the wheel for Mum. As always, she gave in, she understood. Mothers are such amazing creatures. And mine was simply perfect. She was my rock and I can't be more grateful that God chose her to be my mother... I can't even begin to imagine otherwise…

***

We were all ready at Dublin airport a week later, three Indians and a white man ... me. Two of the guys,

Piyush and Sushant kept giving me lots of advice and it started to agitate me. However Sadru agreed with them.

The first few days I felt like I was being bullied but maybe they were just trying to help me. I was amazed at how organised they were and how they kept an eye on me as Sadru had probably told the other two that I had schizophrenia. I think they were very worried about me more because of this knowledge.

Though I was well over the worst, but probably what I didn't realize was the word, '*schizophrenia'* had possibly frightened them. I wish I could tell them; schizophrenic minds may be hazy but we are not crazy.

Instead, I just smiled looking forward to my limited freedom and stay in India…

***

One of the main tasks during my two weeks' stay in India was for the four of us to do outreach to extremely deprived people in Pathankot. The disparity between rich and poor in Pathankot was startling. On the way out of Pathankot, we passed massive mansions and extremely wealthy people and two miles further, we came to shanty towns where there were no toilets and people lived on the tin roofs.

I became very emotional when I saw the poverty there, although Sadru had warned me that it would affect me emotionally but I still wanted to go and see it for myself. I went around like Bill Gates giving out money to the awfully poor as the tears streamed down my face. Sadru told me not to give out all the cash and end up having no money for our own food. He also reminded me that we needed cash for other projects. As in the van, we had loads of food for these people, who were really suffering. Even though I have suffered with schizophrenia myself for years, I could not imagine the suffering of these people living in extreme dearth of the basic necessities.

All four of us went around visiting the various families asking if there was anything we could do to lessen their suffering, e.g. by calling the doctor and paying the bills and asking if there was any medication that they needed and also giving some cash for food and clothing. Personally, I gave one courier €20. He lived in the camp and told me he earned only €12 a month. What should I say; as they weren't even houses, just rooms with roofs of tin, at least ten of them tied down together to accommodate several women and children.

I wondered where were all the men and I asked one of the women and her response was astonishing. She said, “they’re all depressed with life and are gone drinking.”

Also, I had a job to do. Sadru asked me to get the big industrial box of biscuits out of the back of the van and to stand in the field and call the children. Within one minute, there were about 300 children surrounding me all smiling and all happy. I said to the children, ‘now boys and girls, three biscuits each.’ There were 1000 biscuits in the box and 300 children to feed. I proceeded to hand them three biscuits each but some of them looked very hungry so they would get a fourth biscuit.

The whole experience opened my eyes to other kinds of suffering in this world and also made me realize that in spite of my own problems, I was still lucky in a lots of ways and that could have been the moment when I truly decided to look at the worst and be grateful in comparison to what I have.

Spare a Thought

For the Physically ill

I have spent this whole book talking and talking about psychiatric illness. This may be my area but spare a thought for the main form of illness out there in society i.e. 'physical illness.' I have to think of tens of thousands of people who suffer from dreadful ailments and are hospitalized for long months on and off for years. When you think of illness in general, it's very frightening to see people lying sick in bed because there are so many illnesses out there and anyone of us could get absolutely any of these at any time whatsoever.

I always thought that God would strike me down with physical sickness for going to ladies of the night and with my mental illness, I'm probably a bit of a hypochondriac but the thought of severe physical illness; is terrifying! I suppose everybody dreads this but most people do the wise thing and don't think about it... Luckily, nowadays medicine is so good that humanity can recover from loads of illnesses. I feel however, that ailment whatever the type; probably proves that God exists because we usually only get one illness and there are so many different forms, it's mind blowing. For example, I believe that God has protected me from physical illness all my life.

But stop! What I'd like to know is if there is anything that I could do to help people with severe physical ailments? I get really moved when I see people lying in bed suffering with whatever their share of suffering is. But if they're in severe physical pain, I feel terribly sad for them and I wish I knew what to say or what to do... But we all have our crosses to carry and when you get used to yours and realize that you can cope with it; you wouldn't swap it for another cross. All I can do is pray for the physically ill but then again as the expression goes;

"Better the devil you know"

Thankfully, for physical illness as with mental illness; there are more medications that are coming in the market, and people don't have to suffer as much as they had to in the past.

My Long Campaign

I have spent the last three years of my life trying to get merely five minutes to talk about the plight and the struggle of the people with schizophrenia and what they actually endure.

The Irish state broadcaster had treated me very badly. I spent five years trying to get an interview with them about the plight of the mentally ill but to no avail. Every other radio station in Dublin and north Wicklow has been kind to me and let me say a few words before they checked out what I wanted to say and they knew I had a lot of good and pertinent points to make about this stigma – prejudice – and ignorance regarding what schizophrenia actually is and what are the symptoms and the fact that mostly all of us are kind and sensitive and no danger to anybody. We also have low self-esteem and often blame ourselves for the disappointment we have, which is not even our fault at all.

Every radio station in Dublin has put me on air for ten or twenty minutes during the mental health week and a lot of them have been extremely kind and have had me on numerous times. It is due to their compassion that matched my hopes, I was able to convey the help I wanted to for society to understand the mentally ill better – and to try and give us a chance to function as well as possible in the Irish society (we have largely been forgotten by society.)

***

I wrote to Sharon of 'Skyline Radio'…

"Hello Sharon, how are you??"

"My name is Richard Magee and I suffer from mild schizophrenia. I'm quite recovered now and was fortunate enough to know Conor Brady who was extremely kind to me and gave me twelve chances at interviews over the last twelve years to highlight the plight of people who suffer from schizophrenia. I was diagnosed in 1987. I have done radio interviews with all radio stations in Dublin with the exception of Montrose Dublin 4; who have proved impossible. Every other radio station including yours, have been extremely kind. I want to talk about the plight of sufferers in relation to Stigma, having no Purpose because people won't employ us. Hence the fact that as a consequence we have very low self-esteem. We are feared as being violent and dangerous which is patently untrue unless a sufferer is off their medication and taking street drugs. As one the eminent Limerick psychiatrists said; 'people with schizophrenia are more afraid of you than you are of them.' There have been loads of suicides. There is a huge difference between suffering generally with your mental health and having a psychiatric condition 'a brain disease.' Sorry for going on for so long but 'the job-shadow initiative' was cancelled by the government and although there are catering jobs available, some of these are too stressful for the mentally ill. Our voice needs to be heard. I used to do stand-up comedy before I became ill and so I'm not afraid of the media. Sharon, I'm sorry for the long text but if you could spare me five or six minutes during mental health week, I'd be hugely grateful. I'm not sure how long you're with 'skyline radio' but every good wish to you.

My mobile number is ....
My email is ....
Thank you. Richard.

P.S. I'll be in with 'bay water radio' and Caroline during the mental health week."

***

When you have a disease that prevents you from being able to take part in society in a meaningful way, then you are quickly castigated by most people and you are only left to suffer the consequences. Funny how the smaller stations help out except for the arseholes at Montrose.

The Forgotten People

Bless all the Barmen in Dublin, Cork, Limerick, and the rest of Ireland; trying to raise families on a wage barely making ends meet; working their butts off on early mornings and late evenings. Bless all the bus drivers also who do the same thing, only in a different job. To office workers, to shopkeepers, and to ordinary waged bank staff and building society staff, not the top professionals.

The mentally ill are only able to do these jobs for more a day or maximum a week, although we'd love to feel a sense of purpose and not be jeered by hard-headed businessmen who realistically will take the piss out of us behind our backs. Sometimes they need a laugh, we all do, but what they truly need to realize is that we are real people with a disease and we did not ask for schizophrenia. Nobody would dream of asking for it.

To not be able to go and have fun with your friends for twenty years and to disintegrate socially before people's eyes for no apparent reason and also to be perceived as dull or boring because we can't be spontaneous in the throes of the illness. Know that we'll do anything to be spontaneous like any other person. The sense of pain of the mentally ill is very similar to the pain of the drug addicts. The drugs make the pain go away for a few hours but you have to keep taking them to keep the pain at bay.

Both types of drugs; street drugs and the prescription drugs slowly kill the subject, although the street drugs would probably kill people quicker than the prescription drugs due to the conditions and squalor that the drug addicts live in. For fuck's sake people, the least you can do is try and understand the predicament of the mentally ill and the homeless, people from disadvantaged backgrounds who most of their lives are in emotional agony, like we are… give them a chance before their suffering turns into savagery and try to help them. You can surely help some, if not all and that can make a huge difference.

Also, to the chefs and waiters and kitchen porters, I salute you! You work very hard.

Musical Chairs

While trying to get an interview for about a year with our national broadcaster (Radio) in relation to the mental health and plight of the mentally ill, I had to deal with an old cow. She had fobbed me off and lied to me several times, telling me she might put me on air, and then plainly denying that she had even said this. But I was stubborn enough not to give up, hence my exhaustion didn't just end there. I had to deal with another bitch.

Between these two idiots, two good years were wasted just trying to get an interview about our plight. I wanted to help as I knew the plight better than a person who must have done PhD in Schizophrenia; because I went through it. And that year alone, in Dublin, there were over 20 suicides of people with schizophrenia and bipolar disorders. Not that the researchers would care.

After they were gone, I spoke to an eminent psychiatrist who used to ramble on about brain diseases and the chemistry of the mentally ill, as if we were fucking lab rats. I asked him to help me and he promised he would say a few words to the Broadcaster for me, but like most shrinks, his arse hole was bigger than his mouth. He never did anything for me.

I think that with the exception of these idiots at Montrose, all the radio stations in Dublin have been really kind. A year later, I met the wonderful R, who now rates herself as a top journalist, with her head so far up her arse with arrogance. She's married to some bald wanker and has kids too.

She is the leader of the pack on Directline, who think they are great. I told her about the plight of the mentally ill and her answer was: "Richard, a lot of us have mental health issues."

A week after, two more people committed suicide in South County Dublin.

I apologise to anyone who is reading and feeling that this may be too much of a negative talk, but it is just the truth, not my frustrations. At least people who can (those who also call themselves grown up adults), must take our plight seriously. Because human error is one thing and continual incompetence is another; it's the hallmark of being an 'idiot' and many of these certified idiots work in Montrose.

Mind you, Joseph Duffy – an Irish Broadcaster mostly known as 'Joe Duffy' is a gentleman.

So to cut to the chase; a lovely woman on the switchboard at the Radio gave me all the numbers for Directline and there are five. I borrowed two phones from my friends and also had my own phone. I called the show just as they were going on air, and had the time of my life. Calling them, dropping the calls, recalling them, blasting them with music, and then calling another number, right around the switch. I know this is all extremely childish, but I was lied to three times by one researcher, who told me that she would put me on for 6-7 minutes during the mental health week. But they never called me back. So I rang them and asked why? And all she said was;

"We are very busy Richard, goodbye!" They finally blocked my number. Then I switched phones and confused them and before they would have blocked that number too, I would switch to another phone. This continued to happen over and over again. It was a pantomime for half an hour like the musical chairs. I persecuted them and the researcher finally had to beg; "Richard, please stop."

But here in this book is where I get my real payback with such unkind bastards, alienating and looking down their noses at people with chronic enduring illnesses.

Half the country suffers with their mental health due to various pressures; money conflicts, relationship breakdowns, not getting the jobs and many more. God bless the most hard-working Irish people out there. But the fact is, that chronic mental illness is much more frightening than mere depression and anxiety.

We all have to be looked after, but all the service users want is a day's work to feel some purpose and to top up our disability payment, so maybe we could save a few bob and fit into society and not end up dead. Marriage is not feasible with our illness, we just want to try and survive, and Directline are the biggest shower of bastards as mentioned earlier. I also wrote to some newscasters in the Radio (I won't say the name), although they have teams but I heard nothing.

That day at the Radio, was the 'musical chairs' day, when the Directline clowns ran around like headless chickens trying to find out who was getting at them. Without shame I would say; 'dance you bastards, dance as I roared laughing.'

They have made a fool of me… and now I was returning the favour.

Please note that Directline can help people; provided they can get them on air.

Blessed in Disguise

Anxious vs Conscious

My illness makes me anxious if I don't take my medication at the allocated time, but this is only occasional.

I find my experience of the illness easier after a day off from my medication. However, the honeymoon period doesn't last long.

My conviction that I would have damaged my brain after a couple of drags of hash; comes and goes… I consciously avoid large amounts of coffee in any case.

I'm usually able to cope with my condition quite well and I feel extremely lucky - rather blessed about it and at the same time very fortunate too. For a psychiatric patient, this means nearly impossible. But then again, remember that this has only happened after enduring a lot of suffering for over twenty years.

I may be 'unfortunately schizophrenic' and owing to that, I may as well be anxious most of the times, but the good news is there are also those times when I am fully ‘conscious’ of ‘being blessed in disguise’.

This day and age, I can find times where I simply am able to count my blessings…

Reality

Like many people, I had a lot of hopes and dreams as a young person but as you get older you realise that even if you try very hard, more often than not, you'll be disappointed to a certain degree with the outcome. It's just the way of the world but you have to try to persevere. If you have a few close friends, then consider yourself lucky; because nowadays it's the everyone for himself and every woman for herself formula that prevails!

This is generally true even though there are many very genuine people out there along with the bastards. Nonetheless, the bastards are more in number. Living in a city of millions, you really have to hold on to the genuine ones. I don't care anymore about settling down and meeting a woman. It mainly does not happen for people with schizophrenia and anyway a lot of the escorts I've been to, were far nicer and far more genuine than a lot of women you'd meet on a Saturday night in Dublin. Their lives are dangerous, they risk getting STDs; nevertheless they pay more attention to the sexual satisfaction of their clients than their own health, ending up meeting some very violent ones. Certainly they get paid very well, but what is it worth? It must be a terrible job having sex with men you don't even find attractive and on top of it also tolerate their belligerent impudence.

I've often offered the girl 100 bucks for a French kiss and a petting session if they didn't want the full Monty, and the girls have always been so kind as to have sex with me. I'm not Colin Farrell, but I'm kind and caring. However, I shouldn't put myself down. I keep telling this to myself now more often than before that 'I'm a gentleman' and that's what we all should do. Why undervalue yourself when you are as much God's creation as anybody normal?

I wasn't prepared to go through life with no sex after all I have suffered. Thirty-four years of battling anxiety and delusions, watching all my mates settle and have families, while I suffered in a day centre working with black bags and boxes of washing powder. I watched so many patients die from suicide and after all that I couldn't even meet a woman as a friend. The good thing is I had the money so I went to ladies of the night, lots of them. I don't know how many of you would understand but my wonderful counsellor surely understood and understood it well. She wasn't disgusted with me or viewed me as some kind of pervert. I now go to one girl all the time and we are friends.

I feel God only helps when he feels like it or more so if you deserve help. He's not a 'Mr fix it'. We have to suffer in this world. Most of us. It's not fair that it's not all of us and even though I have sinned; something tells me God understands. If he doesn't, the place I'm going to will be no worse than what I endured on earth from the age of twenty-one to forty-eight and because I'm going to continue to go to escorts as I simply enjoy sex. If some other sufferers had had some sex, they'd be alive today. Luckily, I had saved some money when I was younger.

Certain women will vilify me and I understand their anger but please remember that I have schizophrenia and I've tried for twenty years to meet somebody nice.

Talking to Father

"Father Brian Murphy" I said, "I know I can't pull the wool over God's eyes, and I can't just say that I'll repent later and that I know he'll forgive me."

I knew that's not the way it works!

"I've tried to meet a girl for twenty years. Maybe I wasn't praying seriously but certainly frequently enough. It's perhaps not His will to grant me a girl and I'm sure he knows best. But then, I'm lonely and I also have needs like most people do."

"I'm not going to look at it with the perspective that God doesn't care. I'd say it's up to me to meet someone."

"But my self-esteem is very low and battered and I simply don't have the heart or the courage to meet a girl."

"I just couldn't be bothered going through all the strain of trying to meet someone agreeable, when the girls are seemingly totally disinterested."

"My counsellor told me that they are afraid and they don't know if they can trust a guy. It's not all about the looks, they fairly want assurance that they won't get hurt by some bastard."

I vented my heart out while talking to him about things silently scorching my heart for the last twenty years of my life… and boy, it felt good, I felt relieved!

Father Brian Murphy though sad for me was very sympathetic and that made all the difference.

Corona Virus - Hell Broke Loose

Wake up People

When the Coronavirus, Covid-19 arrived, we witnessed it causing hell, but the question is what did we learn from it?

It was possibly the most astounding and shocking challenge for humankind ever! Speaking of which, isn't it remarkable how ONE VIRUS awakened the BEST Creation of God, measuring the vulnerability of a human being at the same time? Who would have thought this out, had it not been for Mr. Clever Covid…!

Apart from the hundreds of lessons most of us may have learnt, my point is: all that medication that the Registrars prescribed us supposedly to fix our delusions *(which they themselves are aware was not the cure per se),* could they recommend any of those to protect themselves though? What's interesting to realize here is the fact that though they are the healthy ones, yet they are the ones now confined. Maybe this will make them understand us better.

Maybe we should all realise that if there is a God, *(and I struggle with it as much as anyone)* we have let Him down badly. We have betrayed Him. We look to science for everything, we try to justify our immorality, saying that we don't believe in God. Some people say *they will repent before they die!* And I just have one question for them … What is the Point?

I have a strong feeling that you can never deceive God. I know that people feel He is not there. It's often so difficult and painful when your life is tough or sore and you're suffering. I know we all suffer in one way or another; however, some suffer more than others, and there's such dreadful injustice in the world, even here in Ireland.

I'm from a middle-class background and I can't imagine the pain of severe poverty but I do wish to try and imagine it!

The way I understand the pain of mental illness, if I ever have the money to help the disadvantaged and the underdogs, by God, I will help them and I mean REALLY HELP THEM! I swear on the Bible, I couldn't give a shit about money as long as I've enough to get by. Of course, many people reading this will call me a hypocrite and a liar. People's patience is running thin in this *dog eat dog* world. Often extremely kind people become cynical and angry because they meet people kind-heartedly but hardly receive any kindness in return.

So often nowadays, when you try to be nice to someone or say something kind to a person, they think there is either a catch or that you want something from them or even perhaps you think less of yourself for reasons best known to you. I make a conscious effort to realise that everyone is having a different day and that some people may be having a dreadful time and that there are a lot of bastards out there *but I am not one of them.*

Poor girls, poor women. Sadly, some of them need men and thankfully there are few good men to make them happy. Perhaps not just enough. Also, I think women are intricate in a different way unlike men. Men are complex too, a lot of them. But women are more fair-minded to men than men are to women, and most of them even appreciate men's company.

My prayer for all the heterosexual women is that they meet a nice man without a very dark side. It's frightful what some women have to endure. However, some women can be quite grim and challenging, often because they've known nothing better except the hurt from men.

Some women need to be kinder to other women too.

I simply wish all the people happiness and comfort for all their suffering.

Why judge the ocean from the shore, why not notice the ups and downs of the waves?

Fuck the Yuppies

It was a Saturday night of March 2020, when Simon and I sat up late grimly watching the news.

The Irish Prime Minister (Taoiseach) Leo Varadkar was saying people were going to die, lots of them, especially older people. All I could think of was my poor mother who now had dementia and was frightened enough and confused by life without having to hear about Covid-19. The poor soul. Philip (my brother) and I swore to each other that we would tell her the bare minimum as she still understood quite a lot in spite of rambling on nonsensically now and again. She didn't need to know too much. We had her safe at home and I would just explain to her that there is a virus out there and that she'd have to wear a mask for a while and keep her two-metre distance from people in the street. Everyone was in the same boat. We'd have to do our best.

Lockdown made very little difference to the mentally ill. We had no work anyway and we spent the day at the apartment; chatting, going for walks and shopping and not working. Schizophrenia had damaged our lives badly. It's not even the fucking illness, it's the fact that you lose too much time to be able to study and you are too heavily medicated to work.

The doctors stuff you to the hilt with medication so you haven't got the energy or the motivation to work. The doctors are bastards. What do they care? Instead of talking to us and trying to be practical and helpful, they give us a fucking prescription and treat us like idiots. A lot of doctors don't even make eye contact with the patient when they are talking to them and can be extremely patronising, treating the individual as intellectually inferior and unable to make judgements for ourselves.

This might be fair enough when we are psychotic, but we recover in time with medication. But they still never reduce it. So we are left incapacitated sometimes intellectually because the medication slows down your brain. I'd love to see those bastards having to take our medication. Yes, we need some, but not a dose fit for a horse.

They merely play us like aerobatics at their theatres (the so-called clinics). Fuck the Useless Yuppies!

The Stunning Alie

And The Wonderful Counsellor

Alie was a stunningly beautiful blond-haired Spanish girl.

I loved her body and began to love her.

She was studying computers and like lots of escorts, she had to go on the game to pay her college bills and her rent in Ireland. Thousands of girls are doing what she had to. Whether enjoying the sex or enduring the sex, they were just regular people who knew they could make €200 or more an hour by fucking men, most of them didn't even seem to mind it.

As usual, I had an extremely low opinion of myself particularly in terms of how attractive I was. I really wasn't. I looked tired all the time from the medication I had to take, I was big and wasn't spontaneous, except occasionally.

I had watched all my buddies get married and have children and progress their careers, while all I had done was suffer in a mental hospital, in a psychiatric day centre for the last twenty years of my life. Be mindful here, that there is a thin line between pity and empathy. I speak to seek the latter for victims like me from society as a whole.

***

Like everyone in life I get depressed now and again but with mental illness, people generally tell me that it's harder to bounce back from a low.

Just imagine for a moment that you miss the key time of your life, without being able to relish any blessings a common man can!

I went to her and told her about my pain. She was my counsellor 'Kate' who would always be as considerate as a true friend. I am so grateful for her…

She was so understanding and always said the nice things and believed that nobody can judge me; as I have suffered and lost a lot of time and that it was understandable. Kate said, "When you feel very down Richard, don't make comparisons with your friends and people who don't suffer with your illness. It'll only make you feel worse."

"I agree with you doc." I said. "Thanks..."

With this illness, often people's dreams are shattered as it gravely damages your life. You can often find it hard to find the will to carry on. And due to these fucking drugs, I am now considerably overweight but I intend to try and get my weight down, though I know it'll be damn hard. But then again, I quote the U.S. novelist John Steinbeck saying in his novel 'The Grapes of Wrath'……

"I know this—a man got to do what he got to do..."

Going running is a huge help to me but I find I have to force myself to go out but it's always worth it. Running can lessen worrying and can break neuroses and all the anxiety about your health. It's a marvellous addition to taking your medication and getting therapy.

Amsterdam

So, here we were after a short flight to Amsterdam. We had booked a hotel called the 'Singel Hotel' right beside the red-light district. The red-light district was the only part of Amsterdam that I was interested in.

Stuart was a born again Christian and as a result he wouldn't go near girls. He was a fundamentalist who believed in the fires of Hell and maybe he was correct!

Years later a priest told me – that was all nonsense and that God evaluated everyone against their story and their journey in life.

"Look Stuart," I said. "Some of them are the biggest rides." I looked at one stunner who was waving me towards her and I could feel the blood rush *(you know where).* I wanted her. But my low self-esteem took over. *I'm not worthy of her, I'm not attractive enough, it'd be torture for her.* Obviously, she'd have appreciated the money. I'd have paid her double gladly, but I chickened out and went down the road looking at other girls. To this day, I regret not going to the gorgeous one. I could have had such a great chat with her before, during and after sex. Eventually, I found the one I wanted. A stunning South American. She was hot.

"Hold my wallet, Stuart." I said. "Don't do it Rich," Stuart said. "God will be angry."

"Aah, He'll forgive me." I said, knowing that if you sin a lot, God cannot forgive you.

"Stuart," I spoke firmly this time. "If you think I came all this way to Amsterdam and I'm not going to get laid, having paid for a flight and accommodation, you must be mad. Now hold my wallet." I said while taking out €60.

"How much?" I asked the girl.

"€40, fuck and suck", she said.

"Great!" I exclaimed, "on top of the €40, I'll give you a tip as well."

"Forgive him Jesus," Stuart was tottering. "He's misguided Lord, forgive him."

"Piss off Stuart," I said. "And stay there, there are far heavier crosses in life, there are far worse things."

To be honest there is very little worse when you're in the middle of you know….

It's for Life

It's Okay Mother

My mother looked at me with sad eyes – and she said that she was so sorry she had brought me into this world with schizophrenia and that I'd had to suffer.

To be honest I have suffered a lot; but at the same time, I've also managed to avoid much of my physical suffering, and that in itself is a miracle.

Occasionally when I was in a bad state, I'd say to my mother, *"this illness is for life, schizophrenia never goes away..."* This was a terrible thing to say to the poor soul. I always apologised to her for saying this. I think over the years I must have spoken these words at least three times.

"I'm sorry Rich", she said, "I should never have had children."

"Don't say that," I'd normally retort, "you've been a marvellous mother overall, you and Dad have given us a great life, in the big picture, you gave us comfort, warmth, shelter and lots of love."

"I only say it's for life when the cross is heavy Mum, I should never say it. I only say it out of frustration with the illness. You're a great mother, it's not your fault, it's an act of nature."

Thank God for the times when I felt perfectly well and positive as well as grateful!

Poor Alan

Poor Alan – Does God care at all? Does anyone care?

Alan had hugely suffered with schizophrenia as I had. It had been three months since I had been in touch with him and all the more reason to feel guilty. He'd never even told his mother that he was diagnosed ten years earlier with schizophrenia.

"How are you Al?" I asked over the phone feeling guilty because I hadn't even texted him for over two months now. I also changed my number and got a new number for the reason that I was being harassed by a girl with severe schizophrenia who wanted to see me every single day for a minimum of a four-hour talk. I didn't simply have the time....

Back to Alan.

"How are you buddy?"

"Arrah, not too bad," he said, soberly.

"I'm so sorry it's been so long. I don't know where the time goes. I've been busy working and helping Mum out and trying to write my first book."

"Arrah, don't worry, Rich. I know you're busy."

But I felt so embarrassed… I'd have to get my act together and call him more frequently.

"How are things in general, Al?"

I know he had serious problems sleeping *(and sleeping tablets didn't work for him).*

"Arrah, never sleep at all, never a minute," he said in his deep Tipperary accent.

"God Al, that's awful," I said feeling very sorry for him. "Is there nothing they can give you to help?"

"Arrah, no. Nothing works Richard, nothing."

"And what about your job Alan?" I asked desperately. "Have you only got one day a week now?" He had told me this before but I still wanted to ask, hoping for something positive for him.

He answered, "Arrah, I've only one full day's work in Elm House *(respite home)*," he said, "and I'm lucky to have it."

"But you used to have three days," I protested. Now I was really worried about him.

"Arrah, I had a row with the other bastard and my hours were cut back by the boss. I've barely enough money to get by." He groaned.

"God, I'm sorry Al…" I said. And I hadn't a penny on me.

"And could you not ask your mother or your family for a loan?" I was distressed.

"I couldn't." He said. "They have no money. My mother doesn't know about my illness and I didn't want to worry the poor creature."

"God Al, she doesn't know???" I asked incredulous.

"No, she doesn't know. I told her I was working on the buildings in Dublin for the last 8 years. Didn't want to worry her...." His voice trailed off at the end.

His mother lived down the country in Tipperary.

"What could she do anyway?" Al asked with pain in his voice.

"Also I never sleep." His voice trailed off as he spoke. "Not a wink! I go to mass every morning at 7:30."

Was God helping him at all? I couldn't help but think. And to me, it didn't look like it.

"I'll try and come and see you soon Al." I said. I was beginning to feel depressed myself. "I'll be in touch Al," I said as if I wanted to reassure myself that I will see him well and happy. I was direly in need of some good news from his side.

"I'll call you next week. I promise."

A week later, I got a call from 'Neville' *(another service user)* saying 'Alan' was dead!

"Alan was dead." I couldn't believe my ears. I didn't want to. How could I? I promised to see him that week, but to see him alive…

He was taken out of Dublin's Dodder Canal at three o' clock on Friday morning.

Another suicide. And for the doctors, JUST ANOTHER SUICIDE!

When would the doctors cop on and listen to us? Will they ever…

Post-Mortem thoughts

On Alan

He had been fished out of the Dodder Canal in the early hours of Friday.

The sun rose but – Alan – gone…

As Dolores O'Riordan of The Cranberries wrote:

"Does anyone care?"

And she, another beautiful, fragile testament to the fact that not a lot of people give a shit about each other anymore.

While meanwhile, the two tweed-suited businessmen strolled down D'Olier Street with their golfing umbrella held high in the rain and as they encountered a poor homeless person, they say to themselves; 'oh I'm alright Jack.' And with and their wallets full of fifty-euro notes; they spared only €2 for the poor – homeless guy with pneumonia and the clothes stuck to his body as he's soaked to the bone and the poor girl across the road with two terrified minors with her; saturated, not eaten a morsel of food for eight hours. Imagine €2!

The last thing they ate was a cold processed burger from McDonald's the day before – with no nutrition in it while that fat arsehole Alikadoo, makes his way to The Gresham for a big, cardiac-arresting feed of lamb chops and French fries and wedge and pints with his peers. He doesn't give a shit, but he'll be in the front of mass the following week, "praying" for the poor and the needy who he wouldn't throw a farthing to.

***

Then of course, Alan was only one of the many mentally ill people to be forgotten about.

Fucking psychiatrists with their patronising comments and their big cars, going on junkets to prescribe certain drugs, often lethal combinations and it seems like some of them don't even read the product authorisation sheets. They simply prescribe the drugs that could sometimes be even perilous when combined!

The Restless Mind

People with schizophrenia have an over-active mind which is constantly flitting back and forward, analysing the past and also worrying about the future at the same time, and they are always trying to stay in the 'now' because they know that they'll be in trouble for not working properly. That's why schizophrenics are in general, unable to work every day.

This then brings in their low self-esteem because they know they can't work as well as the fully well people. What can we do? It's a brain disease, there's not a lot we can do about it except always take our medication, get exercise and try and practice some kind of relaxation technique to ground oneself.

The Delusion

Everyone told me it was a delusion.

I simply could not see this. This illness makes you think and imagine things that are nonsensical.

I had taken a few drags of a joint when I was 19 in a friend's house in Foxrock, and I am still battling this fucking disease. I was at a party and a few of us were standing outside in a porch.

"Hold it in, Richard", the lads advised, when I was taking my first ever pull.

"You will need to take a few drags before you feel it." One of them helpfully added.

I took another pull and then I decided that it was not my scene.

"This isn't my cup of tea." I told my friends. "I don't feel anything at all."

"Hopefully, that'll relax you Richard." One said.

I went home at 2am and fell asleep. I never thought about this incident again – until two years later, when I became ill.

I will have to cry out to God again, I don't deserve anything from God; I often fly into his face; I speak ill of him; I expect him to fix my life all the time. My mother used to say to me, "God is not a Mister Fix it, Richard. He leaves us to our own devices for a reason. The reason being that we have free will in this world."

As Jesus said: ‘My kingdom is not of this world.’

Now, bloody Putin has attacked the Ukraine and it looks like these are the last days of the planet. What an evil bastard he is; he doesn’t care about humanity. But someday soon he will be severely punished.

‘Vengeance is mine’ says the Lord. God help the Ukrainian people.

For those who have absolutely no idea what I am talking about when I speak of ‘The Restless Mind’ – in layman’s terms, the schizophrenic brain operates at about twice the pace of a fully well person. It’s devastating to have this illness but so many people out there are carrying crosses that are worse or as bad. However, they seem to cope better philosophically and emotionally than the mentally ill; because they are already far more balanced than the schizophrenics.

Nevertheless, the good news is – with time a lot of schizophrenics, (on meds and following a healthy life style) become nearly as well as many ‘well’ people.

Goodbye

Suicidal

I had a bad row with my mother over something trivial.

"You're a disgrace!" My Mother said to me.

"In the middle of a recession with a serious mental health condition, you go and lose your job, thinking you're going to get famous doing stand-up comedy!! Such nonsense!!"

"You can damn well do without a phone in your flat now, I'm not paying for it, I can't even claim mortgage protection insurance because you walked out of the job. You handed in your notice!"

"Good God what were you thinking Richard!!?? You're a dreamer living in a fantasy land!!"

It was 1992 and my mother had already put up with her fair share of crosses in her life. She was sick to death of hearing me talking about my delusion and if I had damaged my brain? She didn't understand that

I wasn't well enough to work in the open market and she told me not to come out of my apartment to see her unless I was working.

I'd had a grand job which she had gotten for me. I did the job properly for two years and then I relapsed and began doing idiotic things. I started leaving post across the road for the insurance company there. Our post!! I told the postman I'd do that for him. Madness!! I'd stay in bed late and not come to work if I felt like it. I left an alarm system down in the car park which I was told to keep in the drawer of my desk. Pure craziness!! I had badly relapsed and was totally delusional and I thought I had a chance of getting famous and becoming a top TV impressionist even though I had been auditioned when ill and had badly failed the audition.

She was furious and rightly so. I had a good income and it was a job I could do and it wasn't even a high stress job. I left the house in tears. I wanted to die. I decided there and then that I would take my life and then I wouldn't have to deal with my illness and nor would she... It's a fucking nightmare. You become ill and no one else around you does. You can't function while everyone else can!

'Why??' I cried out to God one night. 'Why have I been chosen for this hell while none of my friends have??'

It's only later in life when I had some semblance of normality when I realised that other people have terrible crosses too, somehow even worse than my cross. There is no justice in this world.

***

The rain dripped from the moss-covered wall that lead down to the entrance of the Park in Cabinteely. I stood there in the rain, crying. The ache in my heart, riddled with delusions and anxiety. Battling thoughts that wouldn't leave me alone. And when I asked the fucking doctors, all they would say was;

"It's part of your illness."

'Thanks very fucking much.' I thought to myself.

After all it had only been a drag, a couple of pulls that had no effect on me. But I was now convinced I had brain damage. My mother used to say;

"Keep busy Rich, it's a kind of a nonsense."

But I really suffered and the prognosis for the future with this illness was not good. The drugs used in 1988 were the Phenothiazines, which were largely ineffective.

I had a plan now anyway. I was going to take my life…

All my mates only gathered around when I was having a bad patch and then they went back to their normal lives and forgot about me. What was my future? Where was my future with this dreadful illness? The doctors didn't know if I'd ever recover – or at least they didn't want to tell me because it takes years to recover.

***

I stood there waiting for the 45 bus to take me back into town to my apartment to be alone. But at least I'd be in peace. I was meant to be going back to Glory Hall tomorrow. After all the dreams and hopes my parents had for me; here I was fucking mentally ill; incapable of working, living on a disability allowance. I'd had a reasonably decent little job at Morrisey Recruitment but like a bloody fool, I had to become unwell and delusional hence I lost the job.

***

There was a neighbour of mine who knew a girl with schizophrenia and the girl tried her best to deal with her illness and couldn't get away from the torment in her mind and like so many schizophrenics, she took her own life.

Sometimes I feel that the suffering is so bad for some, that the reason God doesn't rescue people from suicide is because they have suffered enough and he wants to take them home.

So now it was time for me to leave this fucked-up world. Tomorrow I would take the bus to Dunlaoghaire, bring a large bottle of vodka and go down Dunlaoghaire pier after dark. I would sit in a cafeteria, sip coffee and try to read a paper until after 8pm when there'd be nobody on the pier. That's when I'd go down the pier to the end and sit on the bank and rocks that lead to the water.

I had a load of medication on me and I thought I'd take it down the vodka. I was nervous, but I was really looking forward to dying. I'd be free of all the shit in this life. Dysfunctional relationships, difficult people and the struggle to fit in, when clearly, I didn't. I had done stand-up comedy and had hopes of doing a job in the comedy business; but now I had spent fucking years trying to recover if ever possible. Locked in my head into a disease that most of society feels makes you violent, when nothing could be further from the truth. You are frightened all the time but you are not violent unless you are attacked and set up by some of the scum in society who go around looking for trouble. Not the economically marginalised people but just some trouble-makers who have often no chance to work because they are on drugs.

The next day I woke up still determined to carry out my plan. I went out to Dunlaoghaire on the bus. I had charged my mobile and topped up the credit. So now was the time to get ready to send texts to all my friends and say 'goodbye.'

I went down to 'SuperValu' *(grocery supermarket)* and bought strong spirits. I was planning to take an overdose and end it all because there was no peace from the incessant racing mind and the delusions' attack all the time and I try to rationalise them but you simply cannot rationalise a delusion, it simply can't be done. It just goes round and round in circles.

Firstly, I walked slowly down the pier with a large bottle of *Smirnoff* vodka concealed in a large shopping bag along with a load of tablets. I was now terrified at this prospect but really looking forward to the experience of being gone. I'd had so much pain; I really didn't care about the suffering and damage I'd leave behind. These so-called friends who had their own lives, most of them rarely kept in touch – fuck them all, fuck them!! The only people I was worried about was my mother and my two brothers, also Eoin, Jody, Rob, John, Ivan, Niall and Eamon.

I began to send the texts. First to my most reliable friends.

'Hi, it's Rich. I'm in huge emotional pain, I feel useless. I can't live on. My life serves no purpose.'

'I can't even meet a girl. Every day is hell. I'm leaving this world. I can't go on. I'm destined to suffer. The doctors told me I'd always have this illness and I can't explain to you in words what a dreadful form of suffering it is. They say it could take 20 years to recover and I'm not able to suffer for another 20 years of this.'

I told all my friends I was going to take my life and the calls began flooding in and people telling me to hang in there and Jody, my close friend got scared indeed.

***

The next day I woke up in A & E. I'd drunk half the bottle of vodka and it had knocked me out much before I could get most of the tablets down my throat. I was lucky; I didn't even have to be pumped out. How blessed I was not to have damaged myself permanently. My liver and kidneys were okay. I'd never try this again, I thought to myself. It wasn't God's Will and so I had to stay on earth regardless of the suffering.

***

I've had counselling in the past and some of it was very effective, but I was too afraid to open up to my counsellor about everything on my mind. I have come a long way in terms of recovery from my illness and I had aged quite a lot since I was 33. I was now 54 and I hadn't touched a girl for fifteen years, which is often the norm for a lot of people with mental illnesses as you may be well aware of by now.

Many of those with mental struggles never even get to taste the pleasure of any sexual activity which is often a contributor to the large number of people committing suicide as described in earlier chapters. They simply can't take it anymore…

I'm glad I'm here and I'm glad I'm talking to you...

I needed to talk about my emotional pain, about my sense of loss, about the injustice I often felt when I looked at my peers, me being singled out for this horrible illness. I know you might say ‘what about Africa or the Middle East?’ We have no idea what suffering is. But I had suffered in the mind for 30 years and that had to count for something.

Why don't You Do Something?

When I was in the throes of mental illness, it seemed like I was the person along with the other sufferers, who were the most fun and lucky people in the world. The suffering is intense but the suffering on earth for millions of other people is intense too.

The question is – does it go on for 30 years the way it does for the schizophrenics?

You spend every other day on your knees asking God to help you to pull you out of it and I must say I am tough, because a large number of people who have suffered through this are dead. They are gone with the 'schizophrenia winds'. Like a bat out of hell. Lots and lots of them, disappeared, and people say, *suicide is a permanent solution to a temporary problem,* but how can it be?

I can tell you now, schizophrenia is no part-time illness, it's no three days, or three months of illness. If I knew when I was 10 years old or even in the womb, about what was coming to me in this life; I, Richard

Magee, would have opted out because I spent 20 years in misery – absolute misery! Essentially 25 years of torture and all that over just a couple of drags of a joint!!

But with time, sense, a healthy lifestyle and medication; the worse gradually lessens.

So, these are the common practices in our lives – or should I say our vulnerable existence?

God Forbid, if you are one of the victims of schizophrenia… I promise... I hear you.

Appendix

It's common sense that Medicines are supposed to be our allies during a war against a temporary ailment; NOT a nuclear weapon! I'm speaking on behalf of all the folks with medical psychological ailments. Sadly, there are tons of people with volatile mental health difficulties who lose the most precious years of their lives to the mental ailments.

Speaking of time, the Samaritans are really good listeners but surprisingly haven't a clue when it comes to the mentally ill. For those who aren't aware, Samaritans is the charity that encourage people to be better listeners.

I have never understood what does it take to be a good listener and why is it such a rocket science to let one person complete his say? And also why is it so hard for anyone to comprehend the simple fact that the best way to make a fellow being feel valued and understood is by listening to them without interrupting.

AWARE is a national organisation that helps people with depression to a great extent, through free support, education and information services to those squeezed by anxiety, depression, bipolar disorder and associated mood conditions.

SHINE assists Schizophrenics. They have a varied range of support services for people living with mental health difficulties and their families. However, it is relatively too small an organisation to have a huge impact.

Once again I apologize to women in general for going to the escorts; but it was not out of disrespect for women, just a need for sex after thirty years without it.

"I gasp Awake From Fever's Chill…
As The Thousand Songbirds Sing..
I Ask is it Morning Yet Or Evening Still…
But The Birdsong Sings Its Spring…

–Douglas Hamilton

Made in the USA
Middletown, DE
09 April 2023

28445010R00116